Dear Carol,   3-4-14
Sorry I missey you
     Tonight.
          Best, Kipp

BARRACUDA
IN THE ATTIC

by **Kipp Friedman**

Cover art by Drew Friedman
Foreword by Bruce Jay Friedman
Afterword by Josh Alan Friedman

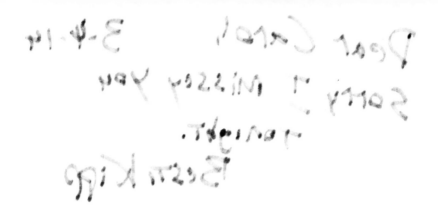

Dear Carol 3-4-14
Sorry I missed You
tonight.
Best, Kipp

FANTAGRAPHICS BOOKS
7563 Lake City Way NE
Seattle, Washington 98115

Editor: Gary Groth
Copy Editor: J. Michael Catron
Covers designed by Jacob Covey
Interior designed by Emory Liu
Associate Publisher: Eric Reynolds
Publishers: Gary Groth and Kim Thompson

ISBN: 978-1-60699-650-8

First Fantagraphics printing: September, 2013

Printed in Hong Kong

For my wife, Anne, who never saw it coming.

The author would like to thank the following for their encouragement and support along the way. I couldn't have done it without them.

My parents, Ginger Howard Friedman and Bruce Jay Friedman; my brothers, Drew and Josh, and sister, Molly; my Aunt Dollie and Uncle Irving, and cousins Chuck and Scott Messing; my mother-in-law Marilyn Foster-Sitter and her husband Elmer Sitter; and my son, Max.

In addition, The author would like to thank the following:

Andrew and Jimmy Franco, Bruce Altman, David Bittner, Rob Sussman, Roman Druker, James Sanders, Martin Swartz, Melanie Wasserman, Lisa Goldman, AJ Jacobs, Larry Smith and Rachel Fershleiser from SMITH magazine, Michael Stein from Filmfax Plus magazine, Mitch Lechter, David Zanes, Hirsh Larkey, Steve Baruch, Steven Dhuey, Shelby Keefe, Ken Eichenbaum, Julie Lesch, Jody Hirsh, Marylee Hansen, Kevin Sullivan, Robert Nicol, Arthur Birnkrant, Walt "Clyde" Frazier as well as crackerjack editor Gary Groth and the entire team at Fantagraphics Books.

Foreword

by Bruce Jay Friedman

Former Senator Rick Santorum (R-PA) is on record as wanting to vomit when he watched President John F. Kennedy's 1960 speech in favor of separation of church and state. I'm no vomiter — are we all clear on that? — but I do cringe when I see the word "parenthood." Or even "parenting." I have four children and somehow I don't recall doing any of that. Nor did I do any homeschooling. I don't see why it's important for my children to hear from me about the rise and fall of the Byzantium Empire. Let some teacher deal with that — while I'm relaxing at some disreputable hotspot.

Did I lead by example? If so, my example was to show up in Vegas, in the south of France, in Hollywood, at Broadway musicals — and to not mind when the boys (and my daughter) tagged along and didn't interfere with my wastrel and sybaritic life.

The word "extraordinary" has been beaten into the ground with overuse — but why should that stop me from using it again? The result of my non-parenting and absence of parenthood somehow resulted in four extraordinary (that word again) children (now adults), which shows you where lethargy and neglect as a parent can take you. Drew, called by none other than Kurt Vonnegut, the Goya of contemporary artists; Josh, with his knife's edge books about America's naughtiest outliers; Molly, quickly becoming a wicked presence on the web — And now, out of nowhere, coming up swiftly on the outside rail, is Kipp with his (Over-used Word Alert) remarkable memoir. Kipp, uninfluenced by anyone, unless it's Huck Finn, with a style as clear and honest as mountain rainwater. What a joy to find out about my own family — and discover I wasn't a disaster as a parent. Maybe I did some parenting without realizing it. (Reverse parenting?)

For all those who feel they didn't do a good enough job as a mom or a dad (there must be millions) I vigorously recommend this wonderful (Over-used Description #3) memoir. And for those who are concerned that they might, in the future, dare I say, fuck up, as a parent, grab this book immediately. And not just because I'm Kipp's proud father. The book is a Godsend for you, for me, and for America — and even for Newt Gingrich.

Important (So I Don't Get Shot)

Let me add that I did receive some help (at least 50 percent) from Ginger Friedman and then Pat O'Donohue, who did some mothering, if not parenting.

1. Life with Father (1977-1978)

Memories of Take-out Pizza, a Wayward Monkey, and the Black Room

My father once asked if I wanted to know the bravest thing he ever did. At age forty-six, he still cut an imposing figure: he was barrel-chested, tall, handsome, and robust from earlier years of weightlifting and more recent jogging — a sort of urban Jewish Ernest Hemingway. He had recently shaved off his salt-and-pepper beard, taking years off his appearance.

Heroic deeds flashed before my eyes. Growing up, I had heard stories of his physical prowess, and, like a good son, I was curious to hear what he felt was his bravest moment.

My brothers had told me numerous times about how he had once lifted a dinner table and thrown it on top of a surly man who had said something insulting to our mother in a restaurant. Then there was the time in the late '60s when my father showed me fresh teeth marks on his muscular bicep. He said Norman Mailer had bitten him in a jealous rage at a party over my father's recent success as a playwright. Mailer had hit him by surprise in the stomach, but instead of hitting back, my father had calmly patted Mailer on his head, saying, "Now, now, Norman. Behave," which only served to further enrage the writer. My dad quipped that maybe he should have had his arm checked for rabies.

On another occasion, our family was invited to a party at Jerry Orbach's brownstone in the East Village that was attended by the organized crime figure "Crazy Joe" Gallo, who had only been out of prison for less than a year. In an effort to soften his image, "Crazy Joe" had lately begun hanging out with people in the theater and arts communities (while in prison, Gallo had taken up watercolor painting and become an avid reader, favoring Dumas, Machiavelli, and the Existentialists). I was about twelve at the time, and I was invited to play pool with Gallo and his bodyguard. Gallo — artistic aspirations notwithstanding — had an active contract out on his life and was only weeks away from being shot and killed in front of his family while celebrating his birthday at Umberto's Clam House in Little Italy.

After the game, he paid my father what he felt was the ultimate compliment, saying, "Your son's a *real* Jew." Brave, perhaps, but my father would later acknowledge that it was sheer folly to have exposed his family to such a risk.

For whatever reason, my father decided not to tell me what the bravest thing he ever did was, which, of course, only served to heighten my curiosity. I decided to let it go. Years later, I brought it up again, but by then he had obviously forgotten. I could see he was searching for an answer that would both satisfy me and get him off the hook.

"The bravest thing I ever did … was … staying as long as I did in an unhappy marriage," he said, explaining that he kept his marriage to my mother going until my brothers and I were emotionally mature enough to handle a divorce.

I knew that wasn't his original answer. Even if it was what he truly felt at the moment, he lacked the sparkle in his eyes that I remembered when he'd asked me years before.

The answer I was looking for was probably overheard around table number four late one night at Elaine's, the popular Upper East Side eatery and writers' salon. He was most likely swapping "Bravest-Thing-I-Ever-Did" stories among his constellation of friends, which on any given night might include novelists, playwrights, editors, reporters, directors, producers, publicists, publishers, actors, police detectives, politicians, socialites, and the proprietress, Elaine Kaufman, as well.

The moral of the story, if there is one, is this: when an author offers to share a "Bravest-Thing-I-Ever-Did" story, don't let him off the hook so easily, for the story might change or be completely lost.

As the youngest son of an accomplished writer whose career has spanned more than half a century, I've heard stories all my life. Over time, many of them have been embellished, altered, and given new meaning. At the risk of oversimplification, my father has always had a knack for taking seemingly random, everyday occurrences and items lifted from the news and allowing his creativity to take over. It's as if he had been hardwired to ask: *what if?* Endlessly curious, he had the habit of wondering aloud whenever we passed a strange town what it would be like to live in there, putting himself in the imaginary shoes of its inhabitants. Before you knew it, he would be piecing together the shards of a new story, and he would scribble down a few notes for future reference.

In the summer of 1972, he was asked to write an impromptu skit for a McGovern-for-President fundraiser in the Hamptons. This was about the time of the Bobby Fischer–Boris Spassky World Chess Championship in Iceland. In my father's imagination, the iconoclastic Fischer — whose erratic behavior was well documented — would begin popping individual chess pieces into his mouth to unnerve his Soviet opponent, thus sparking a Superpower confrontation. He had written the skit on a dinner napkin, and made sure that edible chess pieces were created just for the skit.

In the end, what mattered most to my father was whether it was a good story: something that you'd want to share with your friends, and perhaps even your youngest son. I admit there have been rare moments when I thought it would have been nice to have been the progeny of someone less creative, more practical, with something a bit more tangible to hand down — say, a department store or hotel chain. But oh, the stories I would have missed.

If not the bravest, then certainly one of the most fortuitous decisions I ever made occurred over thirty-five years ago, when I asked to move in with my father at age sixteen. It was the spring of 1977. My parents had recently divorced, and my father was still adjusting to his new single life. He has told me this was a particularly dark period for him. It was also a transitional time for my entire family.

I had been living with my mother on the Upper West Side, along with my oldest brother, Josh. One day, the elevator opened and I saw that it was piled high with stuffed boxes, milk crates, and suitcases. My mother and her new boyfriend, Bob, emerged.

"Bob's moving in," she simply stated as the two of them walked past. Looking like a cross between Carlos Santana and Al Pacino in

Serpico, Bob had long, dark curly hair and a scraggy goatee. He worked for the city's parole office, helping to rehabilitate ex-cons. What I remember most about him, though, was his off-kilter, dopey laugh, because it reminded me of Tommy Chong's. Always good-natured, he would lend me his books on astral projection and *The Teachings of Don Juan: A Yaqui Way of Knowledge* by Carlos Castaneda. We got along fine, but I began to feel like I was an extra wheel in my mother's new life.

They were planning on moving into a smaller apartment on the Upper West Side and Josh, who was now working as a technician at a sound studio, was about to move into his first apartment. My next-oldest brother, Drew, the middle one, had recently returned from Boston University so he could attend the School of Visual Arts and had decided to move back in with my mother. That left me feeling a little uncertain about where I fit in.

I remember asking Drew, somewhat plaintively, where I was going to live, and he suggested: "Why don't you move in with Dad?" Hearing no objection from my mother, I called my father, who gladly welcomed me.

About this time I had a prophetic dream that summed up the rudderless feelings I must have been keeping bottled up inside. I was in the backseat of a World War I-era fighter plane with my mother's boyfriend, Bob, behind the controls, his long hair spilling out of his aviator's goggles and cap. The plane zigzagged wildly through snow-capped mountains while Bob giggled uncontrollably, and I shouted that I wanted to get off because I knew at any moment the plane would crash. As in most dreams, I awoke not knowing the outcome. (Sadly, within a year, Bob would die of a massive heart attack, at age thirty-three.)

When I moved in, my father was busy working on his "Lonely Guy" series of satirical self-help articles, offering important life-skills advice ("what to do with those little left-over pieces of soap") for lonely guys (and gals). The articles, which appeared in *Playboy*, *Esquire*, and other magazines, were compiled into book form in 1978 with the release of *The Lonely Guy's Book of Life*. It would later be made into the motion picture, *The Lonely Guy*, starring Steve Martin.

Recently, I thumbed through my copy of *The Lonely Guy's Book of Life* and instantly recognized a number of things that transported me back to that period of our lives together more than thirty-five years ago. In the book's epilogue, appropriately titled: "Whither the Lonely Guy," he poses the question: "Isn't it possible, then, in some way, to stop dead on a dime and become A Lonely Guy No More?" And then he answers his own question: "Sometimes life itself will lend a hand."

> LONELY GUY (opening door): Jeremy! What are you doing here?
> EX-SON (carrying a suitcase): Hi, dad. I heard you were lonely. I'd like to spend my last year with you before going off to Furman U.
> LONELY GUY: This is an awfully small place.
> EX-SON (entering): Don't worry about it. You'll hardly even notice me. Where do I put my collection of *Iggy and the Stooges* records?

For the record, I never owned any Iggy and the Stooges albums; I was always more of a Neil Young fan.

As bachelor pads go, my father couldn't have picked a better place. His twelfth floor duplex apartment, off First Avenue and East Sixty-third Street, was in the heart of the New York singles scene at the time. *Saturday Night Fever* was spreading the gospel of disco music to the world; you couldn't escape the infectious rhythms of the Bee Gees. Each weekend a legion of satin-shirted, freshly permed John Travolta hopefuls, straight out of Brooklyn and Queens, would make their pilgrimage to the disco-lined boulevards of midtown Manhattan looking for action. One block from our apartment was Maxwell's Plum, which started the whole singles bar craze in the mid-'60s with its ferns and heavy brass fixtures. Around the corner was the original T.G.I. Friday's (long before its omnipresence at malls and frozen food sections of grocery stores), its familiar red-and-white striped marquee visible from my bedroom window. Two blocks south, on Sixty-first street, Rodney Dangerfield still couldn't "get no respect" when he headlined at the comedy club named after him.

Amid the bustle of the local bar and club scene were many family-owned businesses, too — butcher shops, pizza parlors, antique stores, laundromats, hole-in-the-wall delis, Irish pubs, and hardware stores — which lent the area a timeless, homey quality. At the Ottomanelli Brothers meat market nearby, a stout butcher would greet me in thick Brooklynese: "Hey, Bruce Friedman's son! Ya fodda's such a nice man!" while wrapping choice cuts of veal or steak. Even the owner of the Chinese laundromat would tell me, in broken English, how much he liked my dad, while slipping me an almond cookie or dried lychee nut with our laundry.

For over a year I lived in what I would affectionately call the Black Room. My father rented the apartment from a director of television commercials who had painted the walls of the downstairs bedroom pitch black and the ceiling a reflective silver, which allowed you to see yourself (and presumably anyone else you were with) when you looked up from the king-sized bed. The somber color scheme of silver-upon-black gave the impression that you were entering more of a nightclub than a bedroom — all that was missing was a gyrating strobe light. (My dad joked that when he first moved in he found S&M whips and chains in the closet.)

Visitors would ask out of concern, but with a hint of envy, how I could stand to live in such a dark, moody room, but I never felt the least bit melancholy or uncomfortable. The large windows, offering an unobstructed view of high-rise buildings to the west, certainly helped brighten the room, and I enjoyed watching the brand new elevated red tram cable car pass by, carrying commuters to and from Roosevelt Island across the East River. Each night I fell asleep to the whir of honking, braking, and squealing of cars jockeying for position along First Avenue.

My father's bedroom/office area was on the second floor, which led out to a garden terrace, complete with white statuary, overlooking York Avenue high-rises to the east, with a partial view of the Fifty-ninth Street Bridge poking out between buildings.

An immaculately dressed, dour-faced diplomat lived next door. He owned a small spider monkey that would occasionally escape and wind its way down vines onto our adjoining terrace only to urinate in the potted plants. The first few times it happened, my father reacted with mild amusement, but when it continued, I remember his growing displeasure. Fearful of being bitten if he attempted to frighten off the monkey, he would instead coax the creature with yogurt until the unapologetic diplomat would arrive, with a pained expression, to reclaim his wayward pet.

It didn't take long for us to settle into a comfortable routine. I continued to attend a private high school on the Upper West Side and I assumed much of the dog-walking responsibilities. Shortly after moving in, I remember my father asked if I wanted to share a hashish joint in a sort of housewarming gesture, as if to convey that I didn't have to worry about such things. I politely declined (not because I was unfamiliar with such substances, but it just felt funny) and he put away the unsmoked joint and never brought it up again. Rather than set rules, my father had adapted a wait-and-see, laissez-faire approach to our living arrangement. The only restriction I can recall was the same one that applied when I was much younger: try to keep the noise down while he was working. Otherwise, we lived like two bachelors, surviving mainly on take-out food — Chinese or pizza being our favorite — which we often ate while watching a Knicks game on TV.

My father has told me on a number of occasions that he could never imagine doing anything for a living except writing. Sometimes, though, I think that he would have made an excellent chef: he took great pride in his cooking abilities, whether whipping up the perfect French omelet or sautéing veal chops, and he enjoyed sharing his cooking knowledge with me. Many of his cooking techniques, he admitted, were based on tips he had picked up from women he had been dating, and I was the happy beneficiary of these culinary experiments. The trick, I was to discover, was his fearlessness in the kitchen combined with his attention to detail.

Once I had the pleasure of observing him while he prepared sweetbreads, attacking the classic French dish as if it were a science project. I remember him ceremoniously soaking the veal thymus glands in cold water for hours, explaining the importance of removing the blood, fat, and any other impurities. After removing them from the pot, he blanched them with cold water and lemon juice and boiled them to further remove any impurities before drying and flattening them, and then finished the process by battering and frying them in light olive oil. He simultaneously prepared an accompanying Madeira wine reduction sauce. Years later, when I ordered sweetbreads prepared in the same style at several French restaurants, I was amazed at the similarities to my father's one-time concoction.

While he may have been lonely in his newfound single life, he was never really alone. Since his separation and divorce, he had dated several women, and never seemed to lack the attention of many others. The dating seemed to pick up, though, around the time I moved in. As an accomplished playwright, he was accustomed to actors auditioning for important roles. It seemed as if the women he was dating were also auditioning. Once the subject of dating came up and I remember him stating matter-of-factly: "They all want to marry me." But apparently, he was in no hurry to select a new leading lady in his life.

Occasionally, he would ask my opinion about a particular woman he was dating, pointing out an interesting fact about her — one woman, for example, had once dated Clint Eastwood. Sometimes, I would simply offer my thoughts without being asked. Knowing that I was somewhat of a permanent fixture now, I guess the women he dated saw that it was in their best interests to make a nice impression on me as well. But that wasn't always the case. One woman in particular, I recall, made an off-hand comment that my peach fuzz of a mustache made me look childish and immature. Naturally, that stinging remark didn't leave a favorable impression on me (although I quickly shaved).

I did, however, take an immediate liking to Denise, the lanky Wilhelmina agency model who, when first introduced, grabbed me in a tender bear hug (I still remember how great she smelled) and cheerfully handed me a copy of her modeling flier, showing various shots of her in a bikini and wearing a fur-lined winter coat. I'm not sure why that relationship ended, although I remember my father once innocently mentioning something about Denise's overprotective Italian brothers. One positive he took from that relationship, though, was the addition of a delicious veal piccata recipe to his culinary repertoire.

One of the more unusual of the women my father dated was a quiet, unassuming woman I nicknamed "Four O'Clock Franny." I never said much to Fran because she would typically show up around midnight, barely saying as much as a hello, and sneak out the door early in the morning while I was making my breakfast.

Then there was a nurse he saw a few times who worked at a nearby cancer hospital. My father said she always seemed to be a little depressed due to the nature of her work, plus the added burden of caring for an elderly parent. I knew that relationship was doomed when he asked, somewhat rhetorically, whether he could endure a lifetime of terminal-illness-related conversations.

One of his longest on-again, off-again relationships was with Diane, an attractive raven-haired Jewish woman. She was nearly six feet tall and had an infectious laugh. Diane was only seven years older than I was and I always thought of her as more of the older sister that I never had. My father had first introduced Diane to my brothers and me at a

Chinese restaurant when I was about thirteen. While my brothers acted standoffish toward her because of her age, I remember looking up at her in her blue jeans and black leather boots and commenting, "You're tall."

By the time I moved in with my father, Diane was back in the picture. Now at age sixteen, I was painfully shy around women and had a tendency to mumble and stare at my feet whenever women talked to me. So one day Diane decided to offer me some valuable advice on how to talk to girls. Directing me to look into her eyes, she said that the secret to getting a woman to notice you was by establishing eye contact.

A few days later, at school, I noticed a pretty blonde walk by. Our eyes met. But instead of looking away, I returned her blue-eyed gaze, and the most amazing thing happened: she smiled back at me. Diane was right.

As fate would have it, I would run into the same girl while entering our apartment building one day; she lived with her family four floors below mine and I had never even noticed. We became friends and would start traveling together to school. Although a year younger than I was, she had already begun dating.

Several Fridays after school, she led me to Beefsteak Charlie's for beer and burgers, and then, feeling a bit tipsy, we made our way home. Before I knew it, we were back in the Black Room, with me sitting frozen and awkward on the edge of my king-sized bed. The only problem was that I was new to the nuances of boyfriend-girlfriend dynamics; Diane's advice had only gone so far as establishing eye contact and I hadn't the faintest idea what to do next.

After what seemed an eternity, I remember we left and climbed onto the roof of the building and looked out on the city. And that's pretty much how our friendship remained. I may have asked my father for advice and he suggested that if I liked her, I should impress her by taking her up to

Elaine's. Unfortunately, I never got beyond Beefsteak Charlie's, and soon she would move with her family to Roosevelt Island. For all I know, I saw her pass by my window each day on the tram carrying her home.

One of my fondest memories of living with my father was the night we were invited to a Knicks game at Madison Square Garden with Peter Falk, who was at the height of his *Columbo* popularity at the time. We all rode in a limo together, and when we arrived at the Garden, people started noticing Falk and began shouting, "Hey, Columbo!" Falk rolled down his window and assumed his gruff TV detective voice, signing the occasional autograph.

We sat along the center court, just below where the TV cameras broadcast the game, and marveled up close at the basketball wizardry of my childhood hero Walt "Clyde" Frazier and his equally gifted backcourt partner Earl "the Pearl" Monroe. After the game, we continued the party at Toots Shor.

No matter where we went, or whomever he introduced me to, my father taught me never to feel out of place or intimidated by people, no matter how famous they were. He said that if you truly admired someone's — anyone's — work, it was okay to go up and tell them so. I had a chance to do just this when I met Darren McGavin at a New Year's Eve party. In retrospect, McGavin might have been humoring the sixteen-year-old who told him how much he admired his work, especially on *Kolchak: The Night Stalker,* but he seemed to respond with genuine appreciation.

I rarely received direct writing advice from my father, but the subject of writing — and a writer's life — was unavoidable. Each room had bookshelves lined with fiction and nonfiction, and magazines and manuscripts were strewn about the apartment.

He once told me that when Ernest Hemingway was asked the secret to becoming a successful writer, he responded that aspiring writers should begin at "first light," preferably around 4:00 a.m. This was a clever ruse, my father said, designed to exhaust and frustrate an entire generation of potential competitors. This anecdote wound up in *The Lonely Guy's Book of Life,* under the subhead "The Hemingway Legacy."

While I was working on an English paper for school, I remember asking him what he felt was the secret to good writing. He thought for a moment, and then answered: "Specificity" and "authenticity," which made me think of *The Graduate,* when young Benjamin Braddock is advised to go into "plastics." Of course, my father was right (as was, it turned out, the advice about "plastics"), but I had hoped that he would be a little more descriptive.

On most days, my father would get up fairly early, eat breakfast, read *The New York Times,* and scan a few other newspapers and magazines before making his way upstairs to his office, where he would resume his work. With his door closed, I could hear him banging away on his old typewriter with machine-gun intensity. By late morning or early afternoon, he would come downstairs and start the second half of his day. Often he would go for a quick jog along the East River pathway that ran parallel to FDR Drive. For a time I went jogging with him, but he said he liked to use these moments to gather his thoughts and work out problems. After showering, he would emerge in a terrycloth bathrobe and typically pour himself a screwdriver, always pointing out the health benefits of the orange juice. At least once a week he would head uptown to Elaine's to meet friends.

My father typically worked alone, although when he was writing a movie script he would commonly refer to the process as "committee work" because all the people, including actors, directors, and producers, would try to influence the script. While I was living with him, he began working on a screenplay with a writer named Arthur Birnkrant. Arthur had approached him in a deli a few years earlier, not long after my father's novella *Our Lady of the Lockers* was published as a cover story in *New York Magazine*. He recognized my father from a drawing that accompanied the article, and over time he finally convinced him to collaborate on a screenplay of that story.

From the start, it was obvious that this would be an awkward partnership. Arthur was a product of old-school Hollywood: short and scrappy, he had a large head atop his bantamweight frame. He was in his late 60s, and he taught screenwriting classes at the School of Visual Arts. He spoke in a slow, deliberate manner as if he were delivering a lecture and you were one of his students, which forced you to practically hang on his every word. Arthur began his career as a lawyer for trade unions in the '30s before heading off to Hollywood in the '40s, where he would be blacklisted during the McCarthy era, effectively shutting him out of the film industry. My father's story was about a gruesome modern-day crime in a health club perpetrated by a homicidal cross-dresser, and I could easily imagine Arthur stubbornly advocating to insert New Deal-era, socialist themes into the script.

Ultimately, their collaboration would not result in a film, but I became friends with Arthur and would occasionally visit him and his wife, Ruth, in their tidy, book-lined apartment on East Sixty-second Street. The last time I saw Arthur was when I visited him at the sprawling Rusk Institute of Rehabilitation Medicine on First Avenue. He told me that he saw the screenplay he was working on with my father as a final chance at redemption from an industry that had turned its back on him. His body was now riddled with cancer, and he lay in bed hooked up to a series of IV tubes. In a faint voice, he said he had dreamt of himself as a boxer who was given a final shot at the title, and he came out swinging "like a tiger." (Later, my father told me that Arthur had fought to include his boxing "like a tiger" vision in the screenplay as a metaphor for the struggle of the common man over life's injustices.)

I recently rediscovered a college letter of recommendation that Arthur was kind enough to write on my behalf. In summing up my attributes, he wrote: "He is endlessly curious about life, especially our species ... He is gritty, but not gaudily so. He is witty, but understates it." He ended the letter with: "P.S. Lest the reader of this litany worry about saddling the school with a person of virtue, please rest assured that Kipp's potential for mischief is unimpaired, and that he is as vulnerable and as subject to the 'discontents of civilization' as the next fellow."

Arthur was gritty and witty, too. And I wouldn't be surprised if he had fought to include references to the "discontents of civilization" in the screenplay he was working on with my father. As a graduation present, Arthur had given me the complete works of William Shakespeare, which occupies a coveted position on my bookshelf.

During the late summer of 1977, I joined my father on a business trip to Martha's Vineyard, where he would continue to work on the screenplay with Arthur. The Birnkrants were staying in a charming cottage linked to a rocky beach by a scenic, winding path overlooking

Nantucket Sound. We stayed in a nearby cottage, and I would hit the beach while my father and Arthur continued to spar over their screenplay.

Arthur fought with my father to include anachronistic comments in the screenplay, like a street paperboy shouting "Wuxtry! Wuxtry! Read all about it!" which was the 1930s vernacular for "Extra! Extra!" My father would excise such comments from the screenplay, only to find that Arthur had penciled back in the "Wuxtry! Wuxtry!"

"Wuxtry stays," Arthur insisted.

The Birnkrants lived modestly and I sensed the tension that was brewing between my father and Arthur over their project. One day they had us over for lunch, and Arthur's wife, Ruth, made a big deal out of the food. "We have bread," she remarked, with the wide-eyed stare of a religious zealot. "We have butter. And we have salad." My father and I nodded our approval. Fortunately, they also had New England clam chowder.

After they were finished for the day, my father and I would explore the island, including the fishing village where scenes from *Jaws* were filmed, and the more commercial district of Edgartown. At night, we dined on fresh lobster and New England clam chowder. One morning, we were greeted outside our cottage by a distraught elderly lady in her bathrobe, informing us in a choked-up voice, "The King is dead." That's how we learned Elvis Presley had just passed away.

Martha's Vineyard was renowned for its summer parties with the titans of the entertainment and business industries who summered there, and sure enough, we were quickly invited to the kind of garden party one would find parodied in a *New Yorker* cartoon. There were rumors that Carly Simon, James Taylor, and Neil Young were on the island and might be in attendance. My father had a friend staying on the island — a niece of historian Barbara Tuchman — who had invited us to a late afternoon cocktail party given by her parents, but she had evidently forgotten to inform them that we were coming, a serious breach of etiquette. When she introduced us, we received an icy glare from her mother who, visibly upset, proceeded to browbeat her in front of us. (I remember my father's bemused reaction, commenting that being a best-selling novelist just wasn't good enough anymore.)

During the party, we struck up a conversation with a high-ranking Dartmouth faculty member who, when told I was starting to explore my college options, insisted that I apply to Dartmouth, personally guaranteeing my acceptance there. Balancing a drink in one hand, he took out a notepad and asked for my name and, although tempted, I politely declined.

Later that evening, we ran into my father's friend, still smarting from her mother's earlier tongue lashing. Apparently fueled by too much alcohol, she had driven her convertible erratically across the grounds of her parents' compound, accidentally slamming it into another vehicle, where it remained stranded by the side of the road. After we spent some time trying to calm her down (I remember her tears had smeared eyeliner across her pretty face), she took us to a converted barn where my father's friend William Styron was staying (my father wondered out loud if a Pulitzer Prize-winning author was also deemed unworthy of polite company at the garden party).

By the winter of 1977, it was time for me to start thinking seriously about college. I applied to the University of Wisconsin–Madison largely on the recommendation of my friend in high school Wendy

Gaines (daughter of *Mad* magazine co-founder William Gaines) and because of its exemplary reputation as the number one party school in the nation at the time (two perfectly legitimate reasons, I figured, to choose a school). Arthur Birnkrant had shared his own bit of advice, telling me a story about a renowned music professor at UW–Madison who was haunted by the lonesome sound of trains that passed by the campus, thinking that that would somehow help in my decision.

My second college choice, however, was the University of Colorado Boulder, which led me on another mini-adventure with my father. One of his long-time friends, a struggling writer named Tony Tuttle, said he was on good terms with a woman on the English Department faculty at the Boulder campus who might be able to pull some strings to improve my chances of acceptance. So my father and I packed up our bags and spent a week in Colorado. When we finally met the English professor at her home, she was cordial but slightly confused, and it soon became clear that her friendship with Tony wasn't as strong as Tony had implied. She wasn't going to go out of her way to help.

We took a stomach-churning flight on a twelve-seat airplane to the nearby Aspen ski resort, where we spent the latter part of the week skiing. My father purchased a beige Stetson cowboy hat for me like the one I saw Billy Kidd wear on television. My father had never skied before, and after a couple of days on the slopes, he must have become overcome by the Rocky Mountain altitude and decided to hang up his skis for good. Only when we returned to New York did he discover that he had developed pneumonia-like symptoms from two collapsed lungs.

By early 1978, I had chosen to attend the University of Wisconsin after all. With my college decision wrapped up, the school year seemed to pass like a blur. One morning I remember waking up and declaring that I'd like to visit Israel. No one in my immediate family had ever visited the Jewish state. I can't say exactly what led me to want to explore my Jewish heritage, although I do recall feeling a tremendous sense of pride following the dramatic rescue of Israeli hostages at Entebbe, Uganda, in July 1976 and choking up at the news footage of the rescued Jews touching down in Israel. Soon after the rescue, I remember my father wore a sweatshirt around his apartment that read "Uganda is a Sissy," with a drawing of the rotund Ugandan dictator Idi Amin Dada peeling a banana.

As a high school graduation present, my father arranged for me to participate in a five-week youth tour to Israel during the summer of 1978. Upon returning from Israel, I spent two weeks hurriedly preparing to leave for college and was gone.

The year and a half that I spent with my father went by all too quickly. But its impact remains with me to this day. My father once likened this time together to *Mame*, the play about an orphaned boy who goes to live with his free-spirited Auntie Mame and has all sorts of adventures. In my mind, it was more like *The Courtship of Eddie's Father*, the television show about a widower whose young son helps him adjust to life as a single dad. In reality, it probably was a little of both; I'd like to think that we were able to help each other out during an important transitional period in our lives. He was at an intermission stage in his personal and professional life, and I was on the cusp of adulthood.

Postscript: *Whither the Black Room*. After I left for college, my middle brother, Drew, eventually moved in with my father. In preparation for his arrival, my father thought it was time to paint the Black Room a cheery, bright color. On the night before the painters arrived, his friend Terry Southern (*Dr. Strangelove, Candy, The Magic Christian*) arrived around midnight, fresh from an evening of excess, and decided to crash in the Black Room.

The next morning, the painters arrived and quietly worked around the still slumbering Southern and left without managing to stir him. When Southern finally awoke, he became extremely disoriented from the brightly colored room, wondering how he had gotten there, and quickly made his exit. My father loves that story.

2. The Barracuda in the Attic

In early 1967 my father was sent on assignment by *The Saturday Evening Post* to interview New York Congressman and civil rights leader Adam Clayton Powell Jr. who was living in self-imposed exile at a retreat on the Bahamian isle of Bimini. At least that was the plan.

Recent coverage of the controversial politician's alleged financial impropriety had made him leery of any further harmful publicity. So when my father arrived, the former Harlem-based politician and preacher — who was then spending much of his time out of the media spotlight enjoying sport fishing — was less than cordial and kept him waiting for hours. When they finally met, my father was only granted a few minutes, and before he knew it, the interview was over.

Their meeting ended on a high note with each exchanging cigars, but my father didn't think he had enough material from the uncooperative politician for a story. His editors disagreed and insisted that he write about NOT getting the interview. So that's the story that ran, under the apocryphal heading: "Adam Clayton Powell at the End of the World."

Forced to cool his heels while waiting to see Powell, my father did what any self-respecting writer with some downtime in the Bahamas would do: he went big-game fishing. And much to his happy surprise, he quickly caught a bite. While it wasn't a four-hundred-pound blue marlin like Hemingway's Santiago had caught in *The Old Man and the Sea*, he had hooked a respectable-sized barracuda.

Being that this was his first (and only) attempt at sport fishing, he was quite proud of his accomplishment and couldn't wait to tell us all about it upon his return. Weeks later, when the large box arrived at our home in Great Neck, New York, I remember how he carefully removed the barracuda from its packing, recalling what a struggle it had been to reel in the big fish. It had been treated, stuffed, and mounted on a wooden board, and he proudly displayed his trophy in his office/study in the attic of our home.

I'm pretty sure it was my older brothers Josh and Drew, and not me, who first teased my father that the barracuda looked a little old, pointing out that it was also missing some teeth. Dejected, my father concluded that he had indeed caught an elderly barracuda (not that we could really discern the age of a fish) and that it also appeared somewhat smaller than he remembered when first plucked from the Gulf Stream waters. It must have shrunk, he suggested, during the taxidermy process.

To my six-year-old eyes, though, the cigar-shaped barracuda was quite an impressive catch. It was at least two-thirds of my height and body weight, and I thought it made a worthy addition to my father's office in the attic. I remember touching its button-like black eyes with my fingers and admiring the reddish-silver-blue hues that streaked its frame from gill to greenish tail. Most impressive, perhaps, were its uneven fang-like, razor-sharp teeth, which jutted out from its open mouth, creating the impression that it was grinning maniacally, as if it were having the last laugh.

It reminded me of a picture I saw in *Famous Monsters of Filmland* magazine of Lon Chaney Sr. in the silent horror movie *London After Midnight.* I couldn't stare too long at the fish without starting to feel scared and look away.

My father placed the barracuda on a wall above a burgundy leather recliner where he often read and took cat naps after working long hours at the large oak desk that my mother had bought for him at a rummage sale. A year later, he would set a framed poster from his Off-Broadway hit play *Scuba Duba* alongside the barracuda. The poster featured a drawing of a befuddled-looking frog in scuba gear, while referring to the play as a "tense comedy." Its effect next to the old barracuda made it seem as though the menacing-looking fish and the bug-eyed scuba-gear-wearing cartoon frog were indeed locked in an intense comedic standoff.

Occasionally, I would find my father resting on his recliner to the gentle whirring of a Hammacher Schlemmer sleep sound machine droning from a nearby end table. Invariably, there would also be the remains of a cocktail and a half-smoked Macanudo cigar resting on a glass ashtray. His wood-paneled office retained the sweet, musky aroma of freshly smoked cigars, and he kept a humidor with a stash of cigars in a nearby storage closet. He also kept a minibar in his office with a bottle of amaretto liqueur and J&B Scotch Whisky.

A wooden magazine rack next to the recliner was filled with an assortment of periodicals, some of which contained his most recently published short stories. We'd find copies of *Esquire, Mademoiselle,* the

Antioch Review, the *Paris Review*, *Cosmopolitan*, *GQ*, and our favorite, *Playboy*.

Sometimes Drew and I would sit behind the recliner while my father napped or read and take furtive glances at *Playboy* photo spreads and centerfolds. I don't think my father noticed, or if he did, he didn't seem to mind, but I knew instinctively that this was risky behavior on our part. (We had seen issues of *Playboy* before at my Aunt Dollie's house in Fair Lawn, New Jersey, but my aunt had carefully removed any trace of the offending pictures, leaving behind just the text, much to our disappointment, and no doubt, that of my Uncle Irving and my cousins, Chuck and Scott, as well).

I loved spending time in my father's attic office, partially because of the infrequency that I was allowed entry. While my brothers and I had pretty much free reign throughout our three-story house (and did our best to explore and uncover every nook and cranny), my father's attic office was special and to be approached with more caution and a sense of wonderment. Even my mother, who had initially helped him select furniture and decorate his office, spent little time in his private sanctum, giving him the space he needed to do his writing.

Just getting to my father's office, you felt that you were entering a separate world. Our bedrooms were on the second floor and as you ascended a narrow flight of creaky stairs you left behind a cacophony of noise from multiple TV sets and stereos below. My father's office was located at one end of the attic hallway and he usually kept the thick, unpainted wood door locked. We would have to knock before entering, just as if we were entering a real business office. Often I could hear his rat-a-tat typing and the *ching* sound made by his old Royal manual typewriter as he pounded the keys.

Occasionally, during work breaks, my brothers and I would gather around his recliner as he spun spontaneous stories for us or allowed us to make up our own fantastical stories filled with bizarre superheroes such as flying boys with bat-like wings and monkey boys with special banana powers. Sometimes he would capture our stories on a tape recorder. We were at the preteen age when scatological humor would creep into our conversations and whenever our stories drifted into the territory of bodily function humor — typically involving, for reasons I can no longer ascertain, the exaggerated sounds of constipated Chinese waiters — my father would quickly interrupt: "OK, boys — that's enough of that," and story time would come to an end.

For nearly thirteen years, my father had worked in an office cubicle, editing a series of magazines for Magazine Management Co. on Madison Avenue in Midtown Manhattan. He quit that job in 1966 to pursue his full-time writing career. This coincided with our family's move to Great Neck. His new attic office must have seemed palatial compared to the cramped confines of his former office, which shared a wing with the newly established Marvel Comics and its iconic editor, Stan Lee. I remember whenever we visited my father at his office, he would meet us in the reception area and hand us a stack of Marvel comic books, like candy, including such titles as *Dr. Strange*, *The Fantastic Four*, and *The Amazing Spider-Man*.

One of the nicest features of his office in the attic was a picture-frame window, which took up the width of an entire wall, letting in a steady stream of natural light throughout the day. He set his oak desk in front of the picture window, giving him a commanding view of our expansive backyard.

If you stood at the desk you could see a small garden below, as well as the vines that crawled up the side of our Tudor-style house. Beyond the garden was an open stretch where we played ball games. Capping off the view was a curtain of majestic weeping willow trees alongside a gate at the far edge of the backyard.

I remember how proud he was of a tall Spanish-style carved wooden chair with red felt lining on its arms, back, and seat. A red oriental carpet beneath his desk and chair made the otherwise dark hardwood floor stand out that much more. Filled bookshelves occupied two corner walls, and there was a framed poster of a Spanish bullfighter in the ring.

Beside his desk was an antique wooden chest covered with interlacing metal plates and hinges. It looked like Long John Silver's treasure chest and could only be opened by an oversized golden key. I never saw what was stored inside, but in my youthful imagination, it must have been worth its weight in gold to my father. (My mother had a matching chest in the bedroom, which was filled with Victorian-era clothes and shoes, old movie magazines, and other collectible fashion materials).

Upon entering my father's office, you passed a storage closet where he kept his manuscripts and stories on file in boxes. He also had a private bathroom filled with his toiletries (there was a bathroom in the master bedroom one floor below, but my mother's seemingly endless supply of beauty products and toiletries took up much of the cabinet space). He had taped to a wall near his desk a Long Island *Newsday* front page with the alarming headline: "Madman Escapes." Beneath the headline was a boxed photo of a disheveled Richard Nixon stepping off an airplane during a 1968 presidential campaign stop on Long Island. Although the headline and photo were for separate stories, my father enjoyed the confusing placement; he said the paper's editors were obviously sharing in a private joke while sending a not-so subliminal message to its readers.

He kept a framed picture of a smiling President Lyndon Baines Johnson on the wall next to his desk with a funny inscription made out to him. It was a forgery, given to him by his former magazine editor colleague, Melvin Shestack, who was known for his practical jokes and elaborate pranks. Also on the wall was a photograph of my father sitting at his desk surrounded by all his old magazine colleagues, as a reminder of his former place of employment.

As a preteen, I was oblivious to the pressures my father must have been under providing for a wife and three children in a large house in the New York suburbs, especially after having left his full-time job. But I do remember how our middle-aged live-in housekeeper, Mrs. Sullivan, would regularly prepare a fresh pot of coffee and breakfast for him in the morning, and would occasionally find him still asleep with his head and arms draped over his typewriter at his desk after a particularly grueling night of work. These were the days when it wasn't uncommon for him to write a story or two over a single weekend, which would be promptly sold to a willing magazine by his literary agent Candida Donadio. On one such weekend, when I was about three, he sold four stories to *Playboy* — which paid absolute top dollar at the time, at about five thousand dollars per story — and celebrated his good fortune by purchasing a new MG sports car. I remember my brothers and me stuffed in the backseat of the two-seater, with me in the middle on top of the spare tire bump. I didn't mind the discomfort and found the experience adventurous, like a roller coaster ride, especially when I heard the roar from the engine and felt the sudden lurch of the car as my dad shifted into high gear.

While my father was furthering his full-time writing career in the attic, my brothers and I were being equally as creative and imaginative in our explorations throughout the house, including the rest of the attic. We often played hide-and-seek and other exploring games in the adjoining rooms, closets, and crawl spaces, sometimes at considerable peril.

In 1969, Josh had collected several copies of the *Life* magazine commemorative issue documenting Neil Armstrong's historic walk on the moon. To mark this momentous occasion in our nation's history, Josh, Drew, and I stood beside a window outside my father's locked office. They tied a thin rope around my waist. Lifting the window screen, I climbed through the narrow opening and stepped out onto a slanted ledge. Surveying the backyard landscape beneath my feet, I noticed how small the world suddenly appeared. In my own way, I felt like Neil Armstrong taking his first step on the moon. *That's one small step for man, one giant leap for mankind.*

Standing like a skier on an incline, I nervously inched my eight-year-old frame in the direction of a level surface area on the rooftop by the chimney, just beyond the windowsill; I remember thinking that it would make an ideal setting for a game of box-ball. My brothers ostensibly had a firm hold on the rope, even though I felt little tension on the line. I had faith in them, though, just as Armstrong must have had in his fellow astronaut brothers aboard the Apollo 11.

Before I continued my ascent to the rooftop, I heard a familiar rustling sound as a mustard-colored station wagon with faux wood paneling pulled into our gravel driveway. From my vantage point three floors up, the station wagon looked like one of the beat-up Matchbox cars from the collection I kept in an old shoebox. Standing still, I watched as the car came to a complete stop and out came our middle-aged housekeeper, Mrs. Sullivan, carrying a bag of groceries. This was not good.

Josh shouted from the attic window, "Hel-lo, Mrs. Sull-i-van!"

Startled, Mrs. Sullivan looked up and I waved back at her. When she saw me standing on the edge of the windowsill, the grocery bag crashed to the ground. She appeared as though she were about to faint as she braced one arm against her ample chest and slumped against the side of the station wagon.

In a panicked, high-pitched voice she shouted, "Kipp! Josh! Get down! I'm going to tell your fah-tha!"

"What's the matter, Mrs. Sull-i-van?" Josh answered, and then I felt a tug on the rope as he and Drew pulled me back to safety inside the attic window — our first (and only) roof-walk mission aborted.

On another occasion, the three of us discovered a narrow crawlspace behind the guest bedroom wall at the other end of the attic where our grandparents, Papa and Sophie, used to stay whenever they visited us from Fort Lauderdale. Each of us shimmied our way single file on our backs inside the dark crawlspace, not knowing where the passage would lead us. We narrowly missed scraping our heads against a rusty nail that protruded from the low-hanging ceiling inches above.

The crawlspace eventually led into a hidden room that was partially illuminated by light pouring through cracks in the wall. We figured this was where the home's previous occupants stored their luggage, although in our youthful imaginations we were prepared to encounter anything — from a box of gold coins to human remains. Instead, we found something of equal interest: a Green Hornet toy ring — evidence that children from an earlier era had once played in this very same hidden room.

As my brothers and I grew older, our interests naturally expanded beyond our house and our father's office in the attic. Our time became more occupied by school, after-school activities, playgrounds, sledding down "Food Fair Hill," other friends' houses and backyards, movies, music lessons, Little League baseball, summer camp, girls, and family vacations.

My father's writing career continued to flourish as well, as he found himself traveling more frequently to Hollywood. He would expand his writing of short stories, novels, and plays to include work on screenplays and TV pilots. He would also spend more time in nearby Manhattan. My mother was also furthering her artistic aspirations, first by creating an exhibit of original Plexiglas artwork and jewelry, and then serving as an audition training apprentice under the wing of renowned Broadway acting coach and casting director Michael Shurtleff.

Although there were a number of clues that my parents' marriage was beginning to unravel — with words like "separation" and "open marriage" spoken solemnly and in hushed tones within our earshot — I remained blissfully unaware of their marital strife. Soon there would be talk of moving as far away as Italy to "save the family" — anywhere to escape the "negative" influences of nearby Manhattan and Elaine's, the Upper East Side restaurant and writers' salon where my father often met many of his literary friends. My mother said we would start a new life together and my brothers and I would be enrolled in an international school in Rome. Any plans to relocate to Rome, however, remained just talk as we soon moved, in 1972, to a large apartment on Manhattan's Upper West Side. Several months after the move to Manhattan, my father would move out for good, officially starting the separation process that would lead to their eventual divorce a few years later.

He settled into a loft studio apartment on Sixty-third Street off of Madison Avenue, less than a mile from his former Magazine Management office. He now made due with a cluttered makeshift work area in one corner of his apartment, a far cry from his former stately office in the attic.

The only things I found familiar in my father's new apartment were the *Scuba Duba* poster — plus a poster from his more recent Off-Broadway hit play *Steambath* — and the old barracuda, which he placed above a Formica desk (his large oak desk had been sold in a hectic pre-move estate sale). Time and several moves had taken a toll on the barracuda, which was becoming somewhat frayed and starting to resemble smoked fish that had been picked apart at a bar mitzvah. It was missing more teeth and looked strangely out of place against the cream-colored wall, so one day my father simply tossed it out.

3. The Sensus of the Basis

Moments after reciting the four questions while standing on my chair during Passover Seder at my grandparents' apartment in the Bronx, my beloved grandfather Poppy (Irving Friedman) approached me with what looked like a small piece of chicken in his wrinkled, pudgy hands.

"Kipp-ah," he asked, barely concealing a smile, "Would you like the pipik?"

The sound of laughter filled the room. At age six I had no idea what a pipik (Yiddish for belly button) was, but I knew there was no way I would eat the slimy matter dangling from his fingertips. This question, though, would become a staple at family gatherings, guaranteed to produce a smile — sort of like when my brother Drew and I would fight over the wishbone. But unfortunately, it is the only memory I have of Poppy ever actually addressing me.

That's not to say I didn't know my grandfather well. On the contrary, I can still hear his thick Bronx accent and picture his copper-colored bald head, furrowed brow, and sad brown eyes. Poppy had the natty look of a Damon Runyon character straight out of "Guys and Dolls": always impeccably dressed in a jacket, thin tie, freshly starched white shirt, creased trousers, and wingtips. A cigar was always close at hand and he wouldn't go out without a fedora hat. He had a bouncy way of playing the piano, too, which supposedly had caught the eye of my grandmother when she first spotted him playing in silent movie halls in the early 1920s.

He enjoyed making corny puns and malapropisms, turning words like "homogenized" into the phrase "I homogen-ized saw you last night," and, to my youthful delight, magically transforming orange juice into "orange Jews." While singing "Some day my happy arms will hold you" from the standard "All the Things You Are," he'd stop to ask with a deadpan expression: "How can arms be happy?"

I have internalized some of my grandfather's mannerisms. For instance, I occasionally hold newspapers and magazines in a tight downward spiral — like a relay baton — the way my father told me Poppy did during his long subway rides to his Garment District job in lower Manhattan where he was a "cutter" of patterns for ladies' undergarments for nearly five decades. I remember his distinct, warbling bird-like whistle, which you could hear from blocks away and which my father would also employ to gather us as youngsters. Years later, I would try out the whistle on my son, but could never quite capture the right modulation.

I just wish I knew my grandparents better. I wish I could recall entire conversations, words of advice, wisdom, and life lessons imparted from years of experience, handed down like a trusty compass to guide me through all of life's journeys. Instead, I have only disparate, fleeting memories, based on secondhand accounts and random childhood experiences, like the time my father took us to a pre-release screening of *The Godfather* in 1971 on the top floor of the old Gulf+Western building on Columbus Circle in Manhattan. During the scene where Michael Corleone's young bride, Apollonia, unbuttons her blouse to reveal her breasts, I felt cold, rubbery fingers that reeked of Benson & Hedges cigarettes mixed with a tinge of Shalimar perfume suddenly cloak my eyes. It was my grandmother Nanny (Molly Friedman) sitting beside me in the dark, shielding me from what she felt was content unsuitable for a minor; she would also annoyingly cover my eyes during the film's more violent scenes.

Memories of my grandparents can best be summarized by a puzzling question, my own personal Gordian Knot that has tantalized me all of my life: what is the sensus of the basis?

Those were the words my maternal grandfather, Papa (Joseph Howard), uttered one night in 1968 at the Jolly Fisherman restaurant in Roslyn, New York, during a heated exchange with my father. They were discussing the rough treatment of anti-war demonstrators outside the Chicago Democratic Convention when Papa, who had been drinking a glass of bourbon, insisted with bravado: "The cops should bust their heads!" He then boldly proclaimed that if he saw hippies and anti-war protesters on the streets he wouldn't hesitate to "run them all over."

My father, who was fond of his father-in-law and generally avoided conflict with him, asked him if that would hold true if it were his own grandchildren. Perhaps out of embarrassment or, more likely, not expecting to be challenged by my father, Papa raised his arms in disgust and made a sound akin to "Aaaargh!" as though my father had said something ridiculous.

What happened next took us all by surprise. Papa stood up, his thin, tanned face now a shade of crimson with bulging neck veins, and demanded repeatedly in a slurred voice: "What is the sensus of the basis?" Spittle flew from his mouth as he pounded his fist on the table, jarring silverware and knocking over coffee cups.

I had never seen my grandfather so angry. All eyes in the restaurant seemed to focus on our table. Papa's wife, Sophie, tried to calm him down with a soothing "Joeeeee" while my mother offered the more practical advice to my father, "Don't bother arguing with him." Eventually, Papa regained his composure, but for the rest of the dinner — including the following weeks — my older brothers, Drew and Josh, would pester me with the question, "What is the sensus of the basis?" to which, of course, I had no reply.

I still have no answer to my grandfather's puzzling question. However, my brothers and I occasionally refer to that illogical question whenever confounded, vexed, and confronted by something nonsensical. That, I suppose, is Papa's legacy to us. Although I also find myself echoing his other more pointed term of disapproval: "Nahhhh!" a variant on the old Yiddish expression of distaste: Feh!

Once, during the height of the civil rights unrest of the mid-1960s, Papa's older brother Murray shared with family members his less-than-progressive views on racial integration. "I wouldn't live next to a colored family, and neither would you!" Murray lectured, like a prosecutor making a closing argument before a jury. "They ain't got no cul-cha; They ain't got no class; They ain't got no style…." When my mother interrupted, noting that a black attorney and his family lived in a large house across the street from us, Papa responded with a dismissive "Nahhhh!" signaling an end to any further discussion.

My grandparents came from a time when children were to be spoken to and not heard from. That included grandchildren, who were adornments to *kvell* about with their friends and relatives, and to celebrate *nachas* of joy.

They saw their traditional, old-fashioned ways under attack by the more modern, supposedly progressive ideals espoused by my parents' generation, which, in their view, were the leading cause of most of the world's ills. This generation gap, naturally, would lead to occasional differences of opinion between my parents and grandparents, but my brothers and I knew better than to argue with our grandparents.

Of all my grandparents, I got to know Papa the best. We were the youngest of multiple male siblings and we shared a love of sports and games. He was the youngest of five boys raised by strict Orthodox Jewish parents along Broadway and 126th Street in Upper Manhattan. Papa maintained a trim, athletic build, with even-cropped silver hair, and wore glasses that gave him the stern look of an old-time schoolmaster.

He vaguely resembled New York Yankees shortstop and TV announcer Phil Rizutto and dressed dapperly in checkered sports jackets and bright trousers atop white loafers. As a young man he played semi-pro baseball and even had a tryout as a pitcher with John McGraw, manager of the New York Giants, but was turned down because he was told he was too thin and wore glasses, although he claimed it was anti-Semitism. His dreams of professional baseball dashed, he entered the life of a salesman.

Among the important lessons Papa taught me were how to play chess, gin rummy, and pinochle, and why one should always pour salt on cantaloupe and grapefruit, which, he said, brought out the fruit's sweetness. A favorite topic for discussion was his lifelong love of baseball and his beloved St. Louis Cardinals and his hero, Stan "The Man" Musial. He would call the base-stealing Cardinals star Lou Brock "a credit to his race," especially admiring Brock's business acumen as a florist once his Hall of Fame career came to an end (he had no sympathy, however, for more outspoken "colored" ballplayers of the era such as the fire-throwing pitcher, Bob Gibson, and Curt Flood, who single-handedly challenged the league's no-trade clause and long-held racist attitudes). A preferred topic of debate for Papa was who was more of a gentleman, Hank Aaron or Willie Mays?

Like many of his generation, Papa, a devout patriot who supported President Nixon, had a conflicted, knee-jerk reaction to the changing social times, and here he proved to be a bundle of contradictions. Seeing women in miniskirts and "hot pants" on the streets of Manhattan could send him into convulsions of rebuke, this despite the fact that my mother occasionally wore such outfits, much to his chagrin.

A retired traveling salesman and distributor of motion pictures throughout the Midwest, Papa wore his heart on his sleeve and still cried at Disney films. Despite occasional rants about "coloreds," he had a sense of justice that crossed ethnic and racial lines. Once, while traveling on business in the late 1940s, he came to the defense of a black woman on a bus in a small town outside St. Louis, Missouri, when a white man had told the woman to move to the back of the bus. No stranger to both overt and more subtle forms of anti-Semitism, Papa yelled at the man, insisting that the woman had rights and demanded that she remain seated, which she did.

When it came to the sexual revolution and the emergence of the hippie youth movement, however, Papa was clearly dumbfounded. It was as if the world he knew had suddenly turned upside down. In his eyes, anti-war sentiment was practically treasonous. A proponent of family values, he had once boasted of leading a contingent of retirees out of a showing of *Bob & Carol & Ted & Alice* at a theater in Fort Lauderdale, demanding and receiving their money back because of the film's nudity and profane language. Why couldn't more films be like *Dames at Sea?* he would lament.

He had little patience for the youth of my generation, derisively calling long-haired young men "goils," and you wouldn't dare get him started on rock 'n' roll music, which he proclaimed "gah-bage!" (Ironically, he never seemed bothered by the hair length of his own grandsons; my brothers and I had had Beatles haircuts since the mid-1960s and wore our hair much longer well into the '70s.) Once, at a drug store, he grabbed a copy of *Playboy* off the magazine shelf and started riffling through the pages, tilting it to expose the centerfold. "Would ya' look at this gah-bage? Just look at it!" he remarked, with a pained expression. I strained to take a look, but he returned the magazine to the shelf before I could see the "gah-bage" for myself — but then he hoisted the latest issue of *Penthouse* and resumed his diatribe.

Papa's wife, Sophie, would engage us in more of a semblance of conversation. They had married within a year after my maternal grandmother, Blanche, had died of cancer in 1959, a year before I was born. Originally from St. Louis, Sophie had been married three times before and had an adult son, Charles, with whom she maintained a contentious, distant relationship. She once shared with us how disappointed she was that Charles had dated a "colored" woman, saying that he could have "done better." Sophie, apparently, had a few skeletons in her own closet. One of her earlier marriages, she admitted, had turned out to be a mistake. She said she was attracted to his good looks and the fancy clothes he wore, but on their honeymoon he left her to dance with other men.

"He wasn't a man," she concluded with a sigh, "he liked boys." And then she quickly changed the subject.

My mother repeatedly told us the story of how, when Papa had married Sophie, Sophie approached her at the wedding and asked if she recognized the jewelry she was wearing. When my mother spotted her late mother's diamond ring and necklace, Sophie responded with a smile, "Not anymore. It's mine now." And with that, their relationship remained lukewarm at best. Even though she knew deep down that Sophie was good for her father, my mother did not hide her true feelings about her from us, and I suppose some of those bitter feelings rubbed off on us.

Each summer, Papa and Sophie visited us from Florida for about a week at our home in Great Neck, New York. My mother would point out that Sophie had purchased a new pastel-colored Cadillac, implying that she used her money as a means of controlling Papa. The trunk of their large Cadillac would be stuffed with suitcases and boxes filled with Florida oranges and grapefruits, candied fruit slices, coconut-covered date patties, and other assorted gifts that they had purchased at "farm stores," open-air discount markets that dotted South Florida's farm belt.

Once they gave me a plastic panda bear wall clock with silver sparkles around its eyes and a tail that swished back and forth. Not wishing to hurt their feelings, I placed the clock on my bedroom wall next to favorite baseball cards and pictures of Boris Karloff in various horror movie roles torn from the pages of *Famous Monsters of Filmland* magazine. My brothers and I would help lug their suitcases up to the attic, where they would set up camp in a bedroom suite, hanging suits and blouses on makeshift lines. Pretty soon a rich brew of geriatric smells would pervade the attic space including the aroma of Aqua Velva aftershave, cologne, talcum, and other scented powders, as well as ointments and flowery perfumes. For added privacy, Sophie would hang a bed sheet near the door, apparently leery of prying teenage eyes.

Whenever Sophie addressed my brothers and me, the conversation would invariably steer to the same subject: her preference for boys over girls. "Do you know why I like boys more than girls?" she would ask, her eyes resembling large goldfish swimming in a bowl because of her bifocal glasses. We already knew the answer, but would play along.

Girls, she explained, were more expensive than boys. "Girls like diamonds." She would then tell us that our parents were fortunate to have had three sons instead of daughters, and we would smile back awkwardly, although this close-ended line of conversation usually left us speechless.

Sophie's other preferred topic for discussion was business, and more specifically, the status of her stock portfolio. Despite being the beneficiary of wise investments set up by a late husband, Sophie worried about her finances, fearful that her fortunes could change on a dime. Each day she would avidly scan the business pages and then report on any changes in her stocks.

Her frugality was expressed best one sunny summer afternoon when my mother took us to lunch at Gosman's Dock, a favorite restaurant near Montauk Point, on the southern tip of Long Island. We were seated on the deck overlooking the scenic Montauk harbor, watching the passing fishing boats, when Sophie opened her menu and her eyes registered alarm.

"Joe," she said sternly, "there's lobster tails." I noticed that South African lobster tails were listed on the menu. "Whaaaa?" Papa answered lazily, his head in the menu. "There's lobster tails on the menu, Joe!" she repeated, this time more firmly, shutting the menu and staring blankly into space. I could see anger slowly building on her face.

After a few tense moments, she lectured us on their limited financial means. She was apparently fearful that my mother had intended to stick them with the bill. "Joe and I live on a fixed income, you know," she explained. "Joe only has Social Security." My mother tried to reassure her that she would cover the bill, but Sophie remained skeptical. In protest, she ordered a baked potato and a cup of coffee, and sat silently for the rest of the meal, occasionally shifting uncomfortably in her seat, with the withered look of a migrant mother during the Great Depression.

At some point during their stay, my mother would literally start counting the minutes until their departure. This was usually about the time Sophie would ask her in front of me and my brothers: "Which one is your favorite?" to which my mother would answer in exasperation, "What kind of a question is that?" Undeterred, Sophie would repeat the question, "But which one do you like the best?" My mother would shake her head in disbelief and her voice would rise: "I love all three of my sons!"

Once, my mother came up with a creative way to hasten their departure. Aware of Sophie's aversion to our pet cats, my mother encouraged my brother Drew to place Leroy, a black-and-white alley cat with a Charlie Chaplin-like mustache, on the dinner table. When Sophie spotted Leroy sniffing at the dinner plates, she panicked and left the table to start packing her suitcases. Before leaving for Florida, Sophie would give each of us a hug and a kiss and then insist on us calling her "Grandma." Shortly after, my mother would quickly remind us, in case we'd forgotten, that Sophie wasn't our "real" grandmother.

While we didn't always treat Sophie with the utmost respect, we were wary about how we addressed our paternal grandmother, Nanny, who was more of an imposing figure. She had dyed red hair, a leathery tanned face, wore cat-eye glasses, and had a gravelly, low voice that sounded as if dipped in tar from years of heavy drinking and smoking. In old photos from the 1930s and '40s she resembled a hardened version of Rita Hayworth, and the passage of time had not been kind.

The story goes that soon after my cousin Chuck was born in 1948, Nanny was walking him in a stroller along the Grand Concourse in the Bronx when a neighbor approached, pushing her own grandchild in a stroller. "Molly, what a beautiful baby," her neighbor supposedly said excitedly. Nanny peeked inside her neighbor's stroller and responded in her low, raspy voice: "That's an ugly baby." That lack of tact and her willingness to say what was on her mind pretty much summed up my grandmother.

Nanny and Poppy lived in the same Art Deco-era one-bedroom apartment for nearly forty years on a street that bordered Yankee

Stadium off 167th Street and Sheridan Avenue in the Bronx. By the mid-1960s, their neighborhood was rapidly changing as many of their friends and relatives had left for the suburbs or Florida, to be replaced by a new wave of Puerto Rican and Dominican families. Despite the changing nature of their neighborhood, their apartment seemed like it was caught in a time warp from a bygone era.

Near the entrance, they kept a baby grand piano that they'd bought shortly after they were married in the early 1920s. Original sheet music from old Broadway show tunes filled the piano stand and chair. A shelf in the foyer contained a display of Art Deco cigarette lighters and they kept decorative glass ashtrays throughout the apartment with a mini wet bar off to the side. We typically visited them on the High Holidays or on special occasions, but more often than not we met them for dinner further downtown in Manhattan or they visited us in Long Island.

Whenever we visited them, my father would slip a Don Diego cigar inside Poppy's jacket as a sort of visiting gift. Upon entering, I would marvel at the small alcove at the back end of the narrow kitchen just off the front entrance. This was where my father slept on an oversized chair for much of his childhood until he left for college. My Aunt Dollie had slept on makeshift bedding within the TV console box in their sunken living room.

When I was very young, for fun I would crawl inside the console box and stare at faded cutout images of movie stars like Don Ameche, Hedy Lamarr, Loretta Young, and Dick Powell that my aunt had taped to the walls during her childhood. As a child, I thought it sounded perfectly normal, even adventurous, to camp out in your own apartment, although my father told us that it became increasingly embarrassing as he grew older, especially when he would have to explain to a girl he was dating where he slept.

Unlike my maternal grandfather, Papa, who had retired years earlier, Poppy never officially left his job in the Garment District. We heard stories that Poppy had somehow made a poor business decision around World War II, against Nanny's better judgment, and was misled by his business partners out of an opportunity for a controlling interest in the company, coming out on the losing end. The real story was never fully disclosed, but it obviously left a dark spot on their marriage.

Poppy stoically carried on, however, returning to virtually the same "cutter" position for the rest of his working life. This may have been the cause of his painful stomach ulcers, which kept him on a strict diet of bland foods like boiled beef and kasha varnishkes. My father would say that ketchup was the most exotic food Poppy could stomach. One thing we were all aware of was Nanny's constant bickering, often under her breath. She would berate Poppy over the most benign things but Poppy would good-naturedly just grin and take it, occasionally making a small retort.

Blessed with a quick wit and an equally sharp tongue, Nanny would have excelled in business had she been given the chance, but Poppy was too traditional to allow his wife to work. Clearly frustrated, she spent most of her days at home, often in a bathrobe, except when she went out with her girlfriends. As it happens, she developed a drinking problem, although in those days she was what my parents would euphemistically call a "social drinker." It was said that she would occasionally leave the apartment in her bathrobe, carrying a bottle of liquor, and take long cab rides, unloading all her problems on the cabby as a form of therapy. Poppy was known for taking long lonely walks of his own, often sunning himself on nearby park benches or in the bleachers at nearby Yankee Stadium.

Family get-togethers would sometimes end with us silently stepping by Nanny's sleeping body in the kitchen.

Still, Nanny was very kind to us and always showered us with sweets and gifts whenever we visited, my favorite being a box of petit four Rainbow Cookies from a nearby bakery. She also seemed to carry an endless supply of hard candies in her purse.

Of all of my grandparents, I think about Poppy the most — not for what he said or did, but for how he made me feel. There was something very comforting in his quiet, gentle, steady, dignified — even somber — demeanor. My father once referred to me as "Mr. Mellow" and I'd like to think that that was a character trait that I inherited directly from Poppy. As a young man during the First World War, and then in middle age during World War II, Poppy joined the ranks of the civilian defense as an air raid warden, patrolling the night skies for enemy aircraft that never materialized. I still feel pangs of guilt for once shutting the electric car window on his finger when he ran out in the rain to say goodbye to us after one visit. It didn't help that Drew lambasted me: "Why'd you crush Poppy's finger, moron?"

By the time I was eleven, Nanny was suffering from lung cancer. I remember the final summer that Nanny and Poppy visited us at a house we were renting in the Hamptons. Nanny was drinking more heavily and I remember her scolding me for no reason, which made me cry. After that, I would try to avoid her as much as possible.

One night, my father took us to an old supper club adjacent to the East Hampton public beach. There was a piano player and a singer near the bar. After our meal, my father and Nanny stood and began dancing to a standard that we could hear from the bar. Nanny appeared lost in a dream as she gently swayed with eyes closed while clutching my father, who was slightly overcome with emotion. Within months, her cancer would rapidly spread.

My parents' marriage was also dissolving and we were in our final plans to sell our house in Great Neck so we could move into Manhattan, ostensibly so my mother could be closer to my father's work. Nanny was being treated at Lenox Hill Hospital in Midtown Manhattan, and for a while she would stay in my father's high-rise apartment on East Sixty-fifth Street so that she could be closer to the hospital. When she was hospitalized for the last time, events moved so quickly I never had a chance to say goodbye. At the funeral, my father remarked how the officiating rabbi did such a nice job capturing her personality, as if he'd actually known her. I remember how lost Poppy appeared. My Aunt Dollie took charge of all the funeral arrangements.

Within a few months after Nanny's death, Poppy would also become sick. He was scheduled for what was supposed to be routine prostate surgery. Since children under twelve weren't allowed to visit patients for fear of spreading infection, I waited in the hospital visitor's lounge while my parents and older brothers went to his room. Within a few days Poppy would pass away, apparently because he was operated on while he had a high temperature.

The funeral was held at the same chapel as Nanny's, with the same officiating chaplain. Only this time, my father complained bitterly that the rabbi had failed to capture Poppy's true character. At the burial site, it was one of the few times I ever saw my father cry. As much as I tried, though, I couldn't cry, which made me feel a sense of guilt. I wanted to show my father how badly I felt, too; as if somehow my grief would make him feel better. When we left the cemetery, my father placed a cigar in Poppy's open grave. He said he hoped the cemetery workers would have the decency to leave the cigar.

The last time I saw Papa and Sophie was for lunch at an outdoor Italian restaurant in Manhattan during the mid-1970s (Papa would pass away in the early '80s while I was away in college). By this time, my parents were separated and my brothers and I were living with my mother in an apartment on the Upper West Side. Papa still spoke optimistically about bringing "you two kids back together" even though my parents were involved in new relationships and would soon file for divorce.

The conversation shifted to mundane talk about retirement life in Fort Lauderdale, their fondness for "farm stores," and their various ailments. At a certain point, though, my brothers — perhaps out of boredom — began dripping strands of spaghetti and meatballs from their mouths as if they were in a food-spilling contest. Each took turns trying to outdo the other, releasing ever-increasing amounts of food onto their plates while my mother and I did our best to keep from laughing. Neither Papa nor Sophie seemed to notice. Then my brothers, each with spaghetti sauce on his lips, took turns mouthing bizarre noises and curses under their breath in Sophie's direction, which she either didn't hear or chose to ignore.

It was just another in a series of random, puzzling memories of my grandparents that only reinforces Papa's baffling question uttered so many years ago: what, indeed, is the sensus of the basis?

4. They're Coming to Get You, Barbara!

One gray weekend during the winter of 1968, my oldest brother Josh spotted a small listing in *The New York Times* for a double feature of films and convinced my father to take us.

Being movie lovers — especially of horror films — it was not uncommon for us to sit through double features, which presented an ideal way for my parents to entertain three hyperactive pre-teenage boys on a slow weekend. On similar outings we had seen newly restored versions of *Frankenstein* with Boris Karloff and *Dracula* with Bela Lugosi at the Kip's Bay Theater in Manhattan and Tod Browning's *Freaks* paired with his other suspense film, *The Devil-Doll,* at the New Yorker Theater.

The theater this time was located in the remote, sleepy seaside hamlet of Port Washington, about a twenty-minute ride from our home in Great Neck, New York. The first film was innocuous enough, entitled *Dr. Who and the Daleks,* a campy 1965 British science fiction feature starring Hammer Films veteran Peter Cushing as the avuncular Dr. Who, creator of a blue telephone booth that served as a vehicle for interplanetary time travel.

But the real stars of the film were the evil robotic mutant Daleks. While the plot was convoluted and hardly suspenseful, the Daleks, with their toy-like qualities, captivated me. To my eight-year-old eyes, they looked like colorful spinning tops with an array of shiny buttons that resembled candy dot strips. They had metal stick-like arms that they used for grappling and emitting a dangerous gas (clearly a precursor to "R2-D2" in *Star Wars*). They delivered their eerie catchphrase, "EXTERMINATE ALL HUMANS!" in a distorted electronic shriek as though through an echo chamber. I found it amusing how the actors stood woodenly as the Daleks swiveled around them like slow-motion amusement park bumper cars.

After the good Doctor disposed of the evil Daleks, we made a quick trip to the restroom and the concession stand, then returned to our seats and settled in for the second feature. Josh was disappointed by the first film's lack of suspense, but he remained optimistic that the next feature — with the compelling title that had caught his eye in the first place — would actually deliver the horror goods.

He got his wish, and more. For nothing could have prepared us for the sheer debilitating terror of what we were about to witness. It would prove to be a milestone in the history of horror films.

The film began innocently enough with ominous, cheesy background music as a car is seen winding through the Pennsylvania countryside. A brother and sister are visiting a cemetery to place a wreath at the graveside of their father, when the brother begins taunting her with a childhood game he used to play to frighten her.

"They're coming to get you, Barbara!" says Johnny, chillingly, doing his best impression of Boris Karloff. When he spots a disheveled, lumbering man approaching, he points, says, "Here's one now!," then runs away, leaving his embarrassed and flustered sister alone with the man — who attacks her.

From that point on, the film's tension and horror escalated, leaving us and a sparsely packed audience exhausted and in semi-shock.

One could write a doctoral dissertation on how George A. Romero's *Night of the Living Dead* revolutionized the genre of horror films. First, there was its low-budget, black-and-white raw documentary style, sprinkled with TV-newsreel-like segments, which lent the film an air of authenticity (so realistic, in fact, that when it was later shown on TV it was accompanied by a disclaimer: not that it depicted horrific material unsuitable for minors, but that it was, indeed, merely a film).

The explicit, endless depiction of gore was groundbreaking, too. While zombies had been a mainstay of earlier horror films, here were living dead who resembled your aunts, uncles, and grandparents dressed in bathrobes, stained T-shirts — even nothing at all! — shown disemboweling human victims and gorging on flesh and organs. One zombie reminded me of our fleshy housekeeper, Mrs. Sullivan, in her nightgown — somewhat altering how I would thereafter look at her.

No parental guidance warnings were associated with *Night of the Living Dead*; it simply appeared, virtually under the radar, to an unsuspecting public. Ironically, it would be placed as a second feature on weekend matinee lineups typically geared to children. But this film was clearly not intended for the cartoon set.

Late in the film, in a scene where an ailing young girl in a farmhouse cellar turns into a zombie, feasts on her dead father, and uses a cement trowel to hack her mother to death, my father leaned over to us and said weakly, "Boys, I think we should go." I was frozen in my seat with my knees against my chest. My brother Drew seemed equally paralyzed with fear. But Josh, who would later admit to being petrified, somehow convinced my father to stay, and so we remained for the film's duration.

When we filed out of the theater, it was more out of a sense of relief — as if we had narrowly avoided an accident — than a feeling of having been entertained. Only Josh seemed strangely energized, with an extra spring in his step. He would often refer to his decision to stay as a point of pride, as though he had earned a Boy Scout medal for valor. But I don't think I'd ever seen my father, a barrel-chested man then at the height of his weightlifting regimen, so rattled.

We stopped at a nearby diner for some burgers and fries. It was now dark and our nerves were still somewhat on edge. Smiling broadly, Josh excitedly recalled some of the movie's more horrific scenes, but I could see my father was in no mood to discuss the film's merits. He continued to question his decision to allow us to stay, mindful, no doubt, of the nightmares the film would induce. He accused the filmmakers of using excessive depiction of violence as a means to make a fast buck.

While listening to their debate, it was all I could do to avoid looking at my own reflection in the harsh glow of the diner windows, fearful that I'd find flesh-eating zombies staring back at me. That's when Drew — who had a budding talent for pitch-perfect impressions — said to me the chilling words that he would repeat often over the coming weeks: "They're coming to get you, Barbara!" and pointed behind me. "Here's one now!"

I pivoted to find a man at a nearby table eating a hamburger, the man's eyes momentarily locking on mine while in mid-bite. I imagined him as a zombie and quickly looked away. During the car ride home, Drew repeated the taunt and I imagined the faces of zombies reflected in the backseat window from the car lights along the highway.

Younger brothers are often convenient foils for their older siblings to release their own fears, and I rarely disappointed. When our beloved gray Maltese cat, Piper, was fourteen and starting to fade, Drew would tease me with a song he made up: "Piper's gonna' die soon, uh, uh. Piper's gonna' die soon, uh, uh."

Night of the Living Dead signaled a sudden shift in the horror film genre, that monsters and things that go bump in the night were coming a bit too close for comfort. Like most children of the '60s, I had been raised on a steady diet of bland, cartoon-like monsters and horror films that established a clear line between fantasy and reality. We faithfully watched *Chiller Theater* and *Creature Feature* on TV every weekend for such low-budget favorites as *The Crawling Eye*, *Jesse James Meets Frankenstein's Daughter*, *The Brain That Wouldn't Die*, and other long-forgotten B-film classics. I remember Josh joining me in my room late one Friday night to watch the 1940s low-budget Universal Studios film *The Ghost of Frankenstein* on my old black-and-white TV, which barely caught a grainy signal from a New Jersey station. We plotted out our week by regularly scanning the latest issue of *TV Guide,* seeking movies that were described as "melodramas," the code word often used for horror movies. For some reason I always found the obscure 1950s film *The Red Planet Mars* listed every week, usually around 1:00 a.m. I would forestall playing after school with my best friend Bruce Altman so that I could catch up on the latest exploits of Barnabas Collins on *Dark Shadows* — the first and only gothic soap opera featuring vampires, ghosts, werewolves, and witches. I couldn't resist the haunting siren call of the show's theme song as waves are seen crashing against a rocky shoreline and the dark silhouette of Collinwood Manor comes into view.

I honed my budding knowledge of obscure horror films by studying back issues of *Famous Monsters of Filmland* magazine and marveled at the latest *Creepy* and *Eerie* magazines for their hair-raising covers by Frank Frazetta and their wonderfully horrific stories.

In my eyes, my older cousins, Chuck and Scott, were minor celebrities because they had been featured in the pages of *Famous Monsters* for their award-winning monster models of Count Dracula in his coffin and Dr. Frankenstein's laboratory.

Pretty soon Drew, a budding illustrator, would introduce me to EC Comics such as *Tales From the Crypt, The Haunt of Fear*, and *The Vault of Horror.*

Prior to *Night of the Living Dead*, most horror films had followed a fairly standard and predictable formula, with accepted rules of engagement: you could scare us, even hurt some of the less important characters — albeit, without showing explicit violence or prolonged suffering — but the hero must save the girl and good must ultimately triumph over evil. *Night of the Living Dead* seemingly changed the whole playbook overnight by introducing the concept of moral ambiguity. Zombies weren't bad, they were just following their nature as zombies — and we finally got to see the logical results of their handiwork up close and in detail. And the "good guys" weren't all good, either.

Some have suggested that the film was a reflection of the moral ambivalence pervading the country due to the Vietnam War and the growing gap between our parents' generation and the hippie youth movement. But the message was a whole lot simpler for this impressionable eight-year-old back in 1968: no one was safe anymore, and the days of benign, non-threatening monsters and horror movies with happy endings were over.

As far back as I can remember, monsters, horror movies, and scary stories have played a special role in my life. When I was about three and first moved into a room that I would share with my brother Drew, a life-sized cartoon poster of Frankenstein's monster was taped above my bed, like a housewarming present. At first the poster scared the hell out of me. To make matters worse, Drew had a Frankenstein's monster toy about my size, about eye level from my bed across the room, which was conveniently divided by a line of chalk my mother had drawn to separate us like the DMZ keeping apart North and South Korea.

Our babysitter, Mrs. Sullivan, a devout Catholic, came up with an ideal solution: she christened the monster above my bed "Percy" and said henceforth that he would be my guardian angel. From that moment on, I lost my fear of monsters and started to see them in a more harmless, sympathetic light.

Like most children of my generation, feelings of benign, friendly monsters were reinforced by mainstream media, mainly through comic books and TV shows featuring such innocuous characters as Casper the Friendly Ghost and his cute girlfriend, Wendy, as well as the Halloween Claymation *Mad Monster Party* TV special hosted by the voices of Phyllis Diller and Boris Karloff. Saturday morning

TV lineups often featured campy movie reruns of Frankenstein's monster and Dracula battling Abbott & Costello. Even the Bowery Boys and the Three Stooges locked horns with vampires, ghosts, and mummies. Monster-themed breakfast cereals would soon appear like *Count Chocula* and *Franken Berry*, and then *Boo Berries* — each fortified with eight important vitamins — becoming a main staple of my generation's candy-coated diet.

All that seemed to change that fateful night at that remote theater in Port Washington. *Night of the Living Dead* set the bar for the new heights a horror movie could attain, and other films would soon appear to try and match, and surpass, its use of gritty realism.

My main venues for watching many of these new horror films were the old Playhouse and Squire theaters in downtown Great Neck. One particularly disturbing film, which could hardly be classified as a horror film, was *A Man Called Horse*. I remember watching the film in 1970 with my school friend Mark Clark, an asthmatic boy with buckteeth and a nasally drawl. In one particularly gruesome scene, Richard Harris, who plays a Civil War-era Union soldier captured by Native Americans, is subjected to an initiation rite in which bird talons are hooked into his pectoral muscles and he is suspended above ground. Mark literally hid under his seat, his teeth chattering as he moaned in a voice reminiscent of TV's talking horse Mr. Ed: "I'm scared — let's go!" and we soon left the theater.

Later in 1970, I saw *Beneath the Planet of the Apes*, the sequel to *Planet of the Apes*. While this was more of a science fiction fantasy, it raised the specter of nuclear annihilation so convincingly that a theater full of impressionable teens was left in paroxysms of fear. I was sitting in the front row center at the Squire when, during the film's climatic scene as a nuclear device is about to be launched and the evil cult-like leaders who rule the underworld peel off their masks to reveal their horrifically veined, fleshless faces, I went into a form of a seizure and stumbled down the aisle in a sweaty, hallucinatory haze.

After moving to Manhattan in 1972, Drew and I spotted the horror film *Last House on the Left* and convinced our father to take us, this time without Josh. The film was being shown in a dingy theater on Forty-second Street and Seventh Avenue, sandwiched between rows of theaters featuring Kung Fu movies, porno flicks, burlesque houses, and massage parlors. My father, undoubtedly, would have had second thoughts about taking us had he read the film's advertisement which warned: "TO AVOID FAINTING, KEEP REPEATING, IT'S ONLY A MOVIE ... ONLY A MOVIE ... ONLY A MOVIE ..."

From what I remember of the film's flimsy plot, a couple of hitchhiking girls trying to score drugs in Manhattan are picked up by a group of escaped, deranged prisoners and are brought to a house in the woods in rural New Jersey where they are beaten, raped, and subjected to all other forms of abuse. About a third of the way through this ode to sadomasochism, my dad turned to us and said, rather forcefully: "Come on, boys. We're going."

This time, there was no objection from us. As we were walking down the aisles, we had to sidestep an unconscious man sprawled across the floor with his mouth wide open. My father cracked: "Guess he forgot to repeat *it's only a movie.*"

By 1973, my parents were separated and I lived with my mother and brothers in the El Dorado apartment building on Ninetieth Street and Central Park West. I remember feeling somewhat estranged from my suburban upbringing, especially during Halloween, when I would roam the streets of Great Neck at night with friends dressed in monster outfits, knocking on doors and collecting candy. It did not seem wise for teens on the Upper West Side in the early '70s to go trick-or-treating at night. So one Halloween, Drew and I put on monster masks and descended the stairwell of the El Dorado, stopping on each floor to ring doorbells and ask for candy from mostly elderly Jewish residents unfamiliar with the Halloween tradition.

I wore a mask as Tor Johnson from *Plan 9 From Outer Space* and he wore a Frankenstein's monster mask. When we had entered the twelfth floor, we gave a middle-aged woman waiting by the elevator the scare of her life. She had just emerged from a psychiatrist's office. Straining to see through the mask's hot rubbery slits, I noticed the woman emit a faint shriek as she recoiled in terror against a wall.

Hearing the commotion, her psychiatrist rushed out into the hallway to comfort her with one arm, while shooing us away with his free hand as if we were bothersome gnats. As we made our way up the stairwell, Drew and I speculated that the psychiatrist had just finished counseling the women about her continuing neuroses: "there's nothing to fear … there's nothing for you to be afraid of…" when we had showed up.

But the woman's terrified response took the fun out of our trick-or-treating, and we made a hasty retreat to our apartment, disappointed with our overall take of candy.

Soon another new obscure horror film would catch our attention: *The Texas Chainsaw Massacre*, which was playing as a double feature with the Bruce Lee Kung Fu blockbuster *Enter the Dragon* in Times Square. This time, Josh had the good sense not to bother inviting our father. Instead, it was just the three of us. We were aware of the film's growing reputation and wanted — *had* — to see if it lived up to the hype as being even scarier than *Night of the Living Dead*.

I was now thirteen years old and assumed that I was no longer capable of being as scared as when I had seen *Night of the Living Dead* at age eight.

I was wrong.

Soon into the film, the three of us were cringing in our seats in a cold sweat. This time, Josh was the one who raised the notion of leaving, but Drew and I convinced him to stay. About midway through the film, though, the strangest thing happened. After witnessing endless rounds of massacre and bloodletting involving cannibalism, people being impaled on slaughterhouse meat hooks, and victims being chain-sawed to death in wheelchairs, we started to hear laughter coming from the audience.

My brothers and I joined in, nervously as first, and then with full gusto. If fear and humor are polar opposites, then we had gone from one extreme to another. There was something strangely familiar about the plot as well, which all of us seemed to pick up on: amid the endless depiction of gore, the film's heroine had managed to survive, and even outwit her pursuers. The film had become a comedy of errors, and seemed almost cartoon-like in its brutality.

It ended with the leather-faced, chainsaw-wielding aggressor swinging his chainsaw wildly at passing motorists along a barren highway like Wile E. Coyote failing to capture the Road Runner with one of his ACME devices.

This was our generation's hapless Frankenstein's monster. And instead of fearing him, we were laughing. But I would not feel the urge to plaster a poster of *The Texas Chainsaw Massacre* above my bed. Nor would I ever go to see another horror film with my brothers again.

5. Our War with the Schanbergs

From 1966 through 1972 there were two Cold Wars: one fought on the world's stage and the other in suburban Great Neck, New York, pitting my family against our neighbors, the Schanbergs (not their real name) in an updated Jewish version of the Hatfields vs. the McCoys.

I was an active combatant in this ongoing dispute — which played itself out primarily in our backyards — and I may have unwittingly fired the opening salvo and laid the groundwork (more on that later) for future skirmishes. Over time, though, everyone in both camps would take a role in this simmering family feud, down to the Schanbergs' beautiful but hyper collie, Putt Putt, whose incessant Lassie-like barking from within his wire cage could be heard at all hours of the day and would keep us awake at night.

Great Neck, New York, had once been a playground to the rich and famous, serving as the inspiration for F. Scott Fitzgerald's *The Great Gatsby*. Only a thirty-minute commute from Manhattan, such luminaries as Groucho Marx, Eddie Cantor, Basil Rathbone, and Ring Lardner had called it home during the Roaring Twenties.

Our move there in spring of 1966 coincided with the arrival of a new generation of middle- and upper-middle-class, mostly Jewish professionals seeking more space and comfort in which to raise their families while maintaining close ties to Manhattan.

My father was on the verge of quitting a Madison Avenue career in magazine editing to become a full-time freelance writer when my parents bought a Tudor-style home in the Village of Great Neck Estates from the heirs to the King Kullen chain. (King Kullen was America's first supermarket.) Across the street from us was a Mediterranean-style red-tiled house where F. Scott Fitzgerald once lived with his wife, Zelda, who, in a fit of histrionics, allegedly climbed on the rooftop and could only be extricated by the local fire department. Ring Lardner had lived across the street from the Fitzgerald home, often meeting F. Scott for drinks.

Soon after moving to Great Neck, my mother befriended the current owners of the former Fitzgerald home across the street — mainly, I suspect, so she could take a tour of the home and see the upstairs room where the celebrated author did much of his work. While she was exploring the house, I remained downstairs with their daughter, a classmate of mine, who promptly invited me to play doctor in the first-floor bathroom.

I remember she tempted me with the proposition, "I'll show you mine if you show me yours," which I readily accepted. But when it was time for her to reciprocate, much to my chagrin, she backed out (years later, though, I would employ that line to greater success in college). To my shame and horror, the next day at school she told her girlfriends about the incident, and a school custodian had to literally pry me off her.

Our differences with our other new neighbors, the Schanbergs, started innocently enough, as disputes often do. Shortly after we moved in, we paid them a visit at their gray Colonial-style home with large columns, where the silent screen star Pearl White (of *The Perils of Pauline* serial fame) once resided. A thin row of mature, prickly hedges separated our two properties, forcing us to pass through a narrow opening which led into their backyard.

We met Dr. Seymour Schanberg, an intense-looking short man with a beard who had a psychiatry practice on the Upper West Side of Manhattan, his taller, athletically built Swiss-born blonde wife, Marina, and their three sons. Jordan, ten, was the same age as my oldest brother, Josh. Seth, seven, was a year older than I was, and Reuben, five, their youngest, was a year younger than I was.

For reasons I can no longer recall, Seth and I took an instant dislike to each other. We may have simply looked at each other funny. In the world of children, it doesn't take much for a flare-up to occur, and I was the one who would provide the spark.

Only moments after being introduced, I challenged Seth: "I can beat you up." Seth quickly responded, "No you can't," and we collided like two dogs. We wrestled to the ground, where we continued to tussle, rolling over and over each other in the dirt.

Dismayed, our parents quickly separated us and the fight ended as suddenly as it had begun. But that awkward first meeting would set the stage for future bizarre interactions between our families. Indeed, Seth and I would resume our differences later that fall when he would grab my New York Mets baseball cap from behind. As I repeatedly lunged to grab it from his outstretched arm, he twirled like a bullfighter, causing me to lose my balance and fall on the concrete sidewalk, resulting in a bone fracture in my right forearm. I limped back up the gravelly driveway with stars swirling in my eyes. When my mother confronted Mrs. Schanberg about this, Seth was forced to issue an apology, the sincerity of which was as convincing as a boy claiming the dog ate his homework.

I attended Clover Drive School and would occasionally walk the quarter-mile distance there and back, cutting through our neighbors' backyards, sometimes stopping to pee in random bushes along the way. Once, Mrs. Schanberg caught me urinating in her beloved flowerbeds near Putt Putt's cage. After scolding me, she brought it to my mother's attention. My mother, however, did not see this as such an egregious offense and told her so, further souring any possible friendship between them.

Although both were housewives supported by successful professional husbands, Mrs. Schanberg and my mother were about as opposite as two women could be, both in appearance and in interests. Stoic and a stern disciplinarian, the humorless Mrs. Schanberg was a blonde, blue-eyed Nordic woman who took an active role in the PTA and looked like she'd be comfortable on a pair of cross-country skis. She was even spotted smoking cigars on occasion.

My mother, on the other hand, was raised in Brooklyn and St. Louis and laughed at all my brothers' bowel movement jokes. A former actress and model, she had dark brown hair and a sultry complexion and was not known for her strict discipline. Occasionally, she'd come up the stairs holding a wooden spoon threatening to whack us for some minor infraction, but I cannot recall her ever carrying through with the threat.

While Mrs. Schanberg enjoyed sports and the outdoors, often racing off in tennis whites to a match at the nearby Great Neck Estates Park courts, and was perfectly at home tending to her garden, my mother's preferred form of sport was traversing the aisles at Macy's and Saks Fifth Avenue and meeting her girlfriends for lunch at the Palm Court in the Plaza Hotel in nearby Manhattan.

Like the ongoing Cold War between the superpowers, there were brief moments of détente and even kind, neighborly gestures between our two families, but you could count these instances on one hand. I remember returning from school one day to an empty, locked house and crying hysterically. Hearing my cries, Mrs. Schanberg invited me over to wait with her in her kitchen (naturally, I declined) until the return of our live-in housekeeper, Mrs. Sullivan, who was out running errands. On another occasion, my father cut his hand changing a light bulb while standing on a ladder, and Dr. Schanberg raced over to stanch the bleeding and apply emergency first aid. My father returned the favor by driving Mrs. Schanberg to the hospital after she had injured her arm in a fall.

In the six years we lived in Great Neck, I recall setting foot in the Schanberg house only once or twice. I remember their majestic sweeping staircase, which looked like Scarlett O'Hara's Tara in *Gone with the Wind*. I can't recall any of the Schanberg brothers ever stepping foot in our house. My brother Josh and Jordan Schanberg once collaborated on a haunted house carnival-style ride, which featured a mechanized cart on a rail with menacing surround-sound music. Their plan was to charge admission to the attraction, but they couldn't agree on the venue: naturally, Jordan wanted it in his basement and Josh wanted it in ours. They finally parted ways, and each worked on his own haunted house ride. Neither ride was ever completed.

As far as I know, my parents never had dinner with the Schanbergs, either at our house or theirs. The only formal interaction my parents had with them was when they held a celebratory summer evening party in our backyard garage area. This was in 1968, when my father's play *Scuba Duba* was an Off-Broadway hit and my father thought he spotted Dr. Schanberg lingering around the corner from the theater one night.

In a neighborly gesture, he decided to invite the Schanbergs to the party. My mother set up a bar and food table inside the garage and hung strings of colorful lights. Partygoers gently swayed to the comforting sounds of bossa nova music coming from strategically placed speakers. The normally sullen Dr. Schanberg quickly opened up and got into the party spirit, downing the first of several mixed drinks. He may have been working on a second cocktail when he made an unsuccessful swipe at my mother's breast.

Having missed his first target, he then locked on to my mother's Israeli girlfriend, Bracha, a husky-voiced veteran of Israel's War of Independence who spoke with a thick Israeli accent. Bracha was not someone to trifle with; she had literally hand-dropped bombs out of small airplanes during several Israeli wars.

Dr. Schanberg made a sudden lunge at Bracha and they both tumbled to the ground. When they got up, it soon became apparent that, in his excitement, Dr. Schanberg had emptied his bowels, the contents of which were now streaming down his pants. My father and some other guests quickly escorted Dr. Schanberg and his mortified wife back to their house. That unfortunate incident would forever strain relations between our parents, and the cold war between our families would occasionally flare up, spurred by the oddest of circumstances.

Perhaps the most bizarre instance for me was when a red ball floated over the hedges while I was playing in the backyard with my best friend, Bruce Altman. When I went to retrieve the ball, all three Schanberg boys suddenly emerged through the narrow hedge opening. With military precision, each silently took a position: Jordan first neutralized me by grabbing hold of me, while Seth stood guard keeping a watchful eye on Bruce as Reuben went to retrieve the ball. Once the ball was safely in their possession, they disappeared as quickly as they had arrived.

About this time I became friends with a neighbor boy who was preparing to leave for college in the fall. He lived several houses down the street and he drove a Volkswagen Beetle. I reminded him of his younger brother, he told me, and he used to fret about the possibility of being sent to fight in Vietnam. One Friday afternoon I invited him over to our house. Josh brought out his electric guitar and amplifier and started an impromptu jam session in our garage. My friend began singing into a microphone and my father joined in. Each took turns on current pop songs such as "It's Not Unusual" and "The Girl From Ipanema," as well as older standards like "Misty," favored by my father, who had a tendency to croon. Josh tried gamely to keep pace on guitar. This went on for about an hour as their concert reverberated throughout the neighborhood.

The following morning, around 6:00 a.m., our housekeeper, Mrs. Sullivan, overheard from her window Mrs. Schanberg barking out orders like a field marshal for her sons to get ready for something.

A few moments later, while we were all still in bed, we learned what it was that they had been preparing. They had positioned radios and record players in their windowsills and yard so that they faced our house and, at Mrs. Schanberg's signal, they began playing at full blast a cacophony of orchestral music. The barrage lasted for about ten minutes and then came to an abrupt halt, again on Mrs. Schanberg's order. Afterward, we could hear their celebratory laughter.

Down the block from us was "Food Fair Hill," where children from our neighborhood went sledding in the wintertime. On snowy days, my brothers and I would join the parade of young thrill-seekers who passed by our sidewalk dragging their Radio Flyer sleds, toboggans, saucers, and a variety of handmade contrivances fashioned from cardboard, garbage can lids, and whatever else they could think of that would slide. There were no rules; you simply waited your turn in line to descend the bumpy hill. If you were fortunate, your ride would take you close to the rusty, discarded carts behind the Food Fair grocery store at the bottom; most rides, however, stopped about midway down the hill, which was pockmarked with depressions. Invariably, bottlenecks occurred as kids waited their turn.

While lugging my sled slowly up the hill one snowy day, I heard Jordan Schanberg shout at me to speed up and get out of the way. Ignoring his shouts, I continued at the same slow pace. Not wishing to wait any longer, his brother Seth began his ride and when I looked up I saw him and Reuben aboard their toboggan bearing down on me. I managed to shift my body enough so the toboggan only ran over my right leg, which still caused me to cry out in pain. Soon I started to cry. I could hear Jordan's loud laughter coming from the top of the hill. My brother Josh confronted him, and they soon began trading blows. Meanwhile, Seth advanced toward me from below. My friend Bruce Altman came to my defense and almost got into a fight with Seth.

At this point, Reuben ran off while Jordan and Josh continued to fight at the top of the hill. By the time Reuben returned with Mrs. Schanberg, a crowd of children had gathered around both boys, who were now on the ground trading kicks and punches. For a moment Jordan got the upper hand, and Mrs. Schanberg exulted like a cheering fan at a boxing match throwing shadow punches in the air. When Josh reversed his position, finally gaining the upper hand, her demeanor changed and she quickly pulled Josh off, calling him a number of obscenities I can no longer recall.

When the boys were separated I couldn't help notice, with satisfaction, that Josh had bloodied Jordan's nose. (To this day, I still consider it the noblest thing Josh has ever done on my behalf.)

Following the great "Food Fair fight," relations remained tense between our families. We spied each other warily but basically kept our distance, our prickly hedges serving as a demarcation line. If we passed them in our car, neither family would acknowledge the other with as much as a wave or nod. It was as if we were invisible to each other.

For the final year we lived in Great Neck, the cold war between our families settled into a familiar state of containment — like the two Koreas — with neither side striking any noticeable blows. Perhaps we were suffering from a form of neighbor fatigue. We ignored each other and went about our business. When our house finally sold, we packed up and moved away to nearby Manhattan.

But that's not the end of the story. Years later, we discovered that the father and son who'd bought our house had misrepresented their purposes and turned around and sold it to a developer, who promptly subdivided the property. For almost a year, construction crews tore up the backyard and then built a new house and driveway behind our old house. Word also reached us that the Schanbergs were furious about the tumult caused by the new construction and its potential impact on their property values. This tumult may or may not have led to their eventual divorce.

But only someone of less-than-noble character would take satisfaction in knowing that our family's moving had inadvertently delivered the final blow in our war with the Schanbergs.

6. Comic Book Fever

I can't remember when I first fell under the spell of comic book fever. Perhaps it was back in 1966 when, at age six, I went to see the Broadway musical *It's a Bird ... It's a Plane ... It's Superman.* Following the musical, my parents took me and my older brothers backstage where we met the play's co-star who, still dressed in Superman cape and tights, hoisted me and other children in the air like loaves of bread. I remember feeling somewhat giddy as he swayed me back and forth, high above the ground, while I extended my arms and imagined myself flying like Superman. Here was the *real* Superman, whom I had only seen previously in newspapers, comic books, and on television.

Later, my brother Drew would bring me down to earth: first, by reminding me that Superman was merely an actor; and then, throwing in for good measure that our mother had called the actor who played Superman "a fag." (Drew, who considered himself the voice of reason, had burst my bubble before, when I was around four, convincing me that our middle-aged, heavyset housekeeper, Mrs. Sullivan, wasn't Mary Poppins, or age nineteen for that matter; I would begrudgingly concede that she was twenty-one.)

Neither Drew nor I knew what "fag" meant, but I had associated it somehow with my mother's friend, the renowned Broadway casting director and auditioning coach Michael Shurtleff, who once greeted us at the front door of his Greenwich Village flat looking like a white Aunt Jemima, dressed in a bandana and gingham cooking apron, holding a tray of warm muffins with colorful oven mitts. Drew and I looked at each other and started to snicker, ignoring our mother's glare of disapproval. Besides being a mild-mannered reporter, did the Kansas-raised Man of Steel also lead a secret life wearing bandanas and gingham aprons while baking muffins in a Greenwich Village apartment?

Before I was even aware of comic books, like a lot of preschool-age boys, I had already developed a fondness for superheroes. And perhaps the first superhero who fired my imagination was Gigantor, the space-age robot. Developed by the same Japanese creative anime team that introduced Astro Boy (and later, Kimba the White Lion, and Speed Racer), Gigantor was a huge flying robot with a jetpack attached to his back. A doe-eyed little boy named Jimmy, always dressed impeccably in a tweed suit and tie, controlled Gigantor with a joystick. Gigantor had a distinct pointy nose and narrow-set eyes that registered little emotion; whoever operated the joystick controlled Gigantor, and thus, the fate of the world.

I must have been only three or four when I would watch, mesmerized, probably bouncing up and down on the edge of my seat, while viewing black-and-white episodes of *Gigantor* on afternoon television. I think I was hooked from the infectious conga-tinged opening theme song that served as a clarion call to all viewing children: "Gigantor! Gigantor! Gigannnnnn-annnntor!" (Years later, it was fun to see my son's similar reaction while watching the opening scenes of the *Mighty Morphin Power Rangers,* which was reminiscent of *Gigantor,* only on steroids.) During recess at North Shore Day School in Glen Cove, Long Island, I would lead a parade of preschoolers as we marched across the playgrounds with outstretched arms as I sang the *Gigantor* theme song: "Bigger than big, taller than tall. Quicker than quick, stronger than strong. Ready to fight for right, against wrong. Gigantor! Gigantor! Gigannnnnn-annnntor!"

My comic book fever heated up around 1968. That was when we began a sort of weekend family ritual. My brothers and I would pile inside our father's car — at first, a midnight-blue Cadillac Eldorado (which he regrettably had to return after my maternal grandfather, Papa, threw up in the back seat next to me one night after a particularly spirited dinner out, overpowering any remaining new car smells with the unmistakable sour odor of geriatric vomit), and later his tobacco-colored Mark III Lincoln Continental — and head into nearby Manhattan. We'd usually stop at a "Hot Bagels" store along the freeway on the outskirts of our home in Great Neck, New York. We'd pick up a bag of assorted bagels and bialys — my favorite being thick kosher salt-encrusted bagels — and then continue our journey into the City, the looming Manhattan skyline beckoning from the Long Island Expressway like the Emerald City along the Yellow Brick Road in *The Wizard of Oz.*

Entering Manhattan via the Queensboro (Fifty-ninth Street) Bridge, we'd wind our way downtown to Thirty-second Street, between Sixth and Seventh avenues, around the corner from Pennsylvania Station and the old Willoughby's camera emporium, and look for a parking space. An oxidized green, arched overhead walkway connecting several buildings along Thirty-second Street would serve as our landmark. Just before we reached the overhead span, we would enter an old building and take a rickety service elevator up several flights (on subsequent trips, Drew and I would forego the elevator, choosing instead to race each other up the stairs, the staccato of our eager footsteps reverberating like the sound of gunshots against the stairwell walls as we jockeyed for position). Flush with anticipation, we barged into a large storage room like bulls entering the ring. We had arrived at what we affectionately called the Back-Issue Store.

More of a dingy warehouse than an actual store, the name of the floor-length storage space was Jay Bee Back-Issue Magazines. To my brothers and me, though, it was like stumbling upon Shangri-La in Midtown Manhattan. The space contained a treasure trove of out-of-date comic books, magazines, newspapers, and other assorted memorabilia from a bygone era, all neatly arranged in seemingly endless storage bins.

No one can recall how we discovered the Back-Issue Store. My father claims that he might have first learned about it from Stan Lee, the iconic editor of Marvel Comics. This is a plausible enough explanation since for years they sat near one another at adjacent cubicles, separated only by thin white dividers. My father worked until the mid-'60s as editor of a series of men's adventure magazines at Magazine Management Co., which shared office space with the smaller, fledgling Marvel Comics.

Our parents were always coming up with new, inventive ways to entertain us on weekends — Coney Island and Palisades amusement parks, Ringling Bros. and Barnum & Bailey Circus, Broadway musicals, monster movie double features, Yankees and Mets games, penny arcades like Playland along Forty-second Street, and visits to cavernous Manhattan bookstores — so taking us to a warehouse stocked with old comic books and magazines was something that would certainly appeal to us.

We would occasionally visit our father's office along Madison Avenue in Midtown Manhattan where we were always encouraged to grab a handful of Marvel Comics off the waiting room table. I already knew about the DC Comics superheroes Superman and Batman, mostly from watching television cartoons and the reruns of the '50s-era live action *Adventures of Superman* series starring George Reeves, and the campy mid-'60s *Batman* series with Adam West.

Visiting my father's office was my first exposure to a newly emerging cast of more complex comic book heroes such as The Amazing Spider-Man, The Fantastic Four, Dr. Strange, The Hulk, The Mighty Thor, and The Invincible Iron Man. We'd receive new Marvel comic books literally hot off the press. While I enjoyed looking at the colorful covers, I was too young to pay much attention to the actual stories inside, although I would soon take notice of those same Marvel superheroes — created by the same stable of classic Marvel artists including Jack Kirby and Steve Ditko — when they started appearing regularly in cartoon form on afternoon and weekend television.

Upon entering the Back-Issue Store, we were greeted by a bored-looking burly man with a goatee and his rangy, long-haired assistant who sat behind a beat up, cluttered wooden desk with an old-fashioned cash register. (My father would later make the observation that there was a certain "look" to comic book salesmen: slightly pudgy, somewhat pale

from lack of sunlight, and typically unkempt in personal appearance.)
The Back-Issue Store salesmen would eye us suspiciously, no doubt
concerned that we might cause a ruckus or worse, steal. But over time,
after repeated visits, they would come to accept us as we became some
of their best and most frequent customers.

On any given visit we rarely saw more than a handful of patrons
— mostly collectors in search of obscure magazines — and never
any other children. Narrow, poorly lit aisles of shelves, boxes, and
file cabinets — each with the names of its contents scrupulously
listed on the outside — towered toward the ceiling. Grime and dust
had settled everywhere, and the smell of mildewy paper mixed with
plastic permeated the poorly ventilated warehouse.

Warped wooden floors seemed to creak and groan with every
step. The place must have been a haven for rodents, and most likely
posed a fire hazard as well, but was still nectar to our young noses as
we freely paced the aisles.

I recall finding back issues of *Sports Illustrated*, *Field & Stream*,
Time, *Life*, *Look,* and even *Playboy*, a magazine I was already somewhat
familiar with despite my young age, because of my father's frequent
contributions as a writer. We also discovered, tucked away out of
plain sight, hidden surprises such as nudist magazines — showing
men and women frolicking in the buff while innocently enjoying a
game of volleyball, lounging by a lake, or engaging in other seemingly
innocuous outdoor activities. I may have taken a few furtive glances
inside, but these magazines held only passing interest to my brothers
and me.

There were dozens of other lesser-known and esoteric periodicals
as well, covering a wide range of topics from astronomy to mechanical

engineering, which we would quickly bypass. There may have also been several decades' worth of old *National Geographics*, medical journals, as well as maps and lithographs. We'll never know. Looking back, I regret having never fully explored the entire confines of the Back-Issue Store.

While we roamed the Back-Issue Store aisles searching for old comic books and magazines, my father stood patiently by the front desk, engaging the two salesmen in small talk while keeping a watchful eye on the time. We knew we were on a tight schedule — usually given no more than half an hour — so we didn't waste much time.

We were also on a tight budget, so we tried to be as selective as possible in our purchases. As the youngest, I'm fairly certain there was some pleading and bargaining on my part with my father. Drew and Josh quickly zeroed in on the cabinets containing back issues of *Famous Monsters of Filmland*, *Mad*, as well as some other magazines I can no longer remember. I set my sights on bins containing a seemingly endless supply of old Dell, Gold Key, Classics Illustrated, and DC comic books from the late '40s through the mid-'60s. I preferred the DC family of comics with such titles as *Adventure Comics*, *World's Finest*, and *Justice League of America*, which featured Superman, Superboy, Supergirl, Lois Lane, and Batman and Robin, but I also grew to enjoy *Archie*, *Casper the Friendly Ghost*, and *Richie Rich*.

Regrettably, all of my purchases from the Back-Issue Store are now long gone, with the exception of one item: a sealed copy of the second issue of *Famous Monsters of Filmland* from 1958, which proudly boasted on the back cover as being "the only magazine BANNED IN TRANSYLVANIA." Josh has since unloaded many of his favorite Back-Issue Store purchases, including the first issue of *Sports Illustrated*, which included a foldout with dozens of replica early '50s Topps baseball card cut-outs, including a rookie Mickey Mantle. I suspect Drew has kept very little of his Back-Issue Store purchases as well.

While I wound up not saving any of the comics I collected from the Back-Issue Store, I still have the very first comic book I ever purchased with my own allowance: DC Comics' *Metal Men* #28 from 1967, which I bought for twelve cents off a rack at a roadside convenience store in Amagansett, Long Island, where we were spending the summer. (I also picked up some beef jerky sticks with the remainder of my twenty-five-cent allowance.) The cover depicted the alloy superhero robots made of gold, lead, iron, mercury, and tin hovering dangerously above a boiling smelter while Tina, the sexy platinum Metal Woman, protected them from being totally submerged in the molten brew. I'm not even sure if I actually read the comic book; like a lot of children, I was probably simply drawn to the colorful cover artwork. Often, the stories did not live up to the expectation created by the sensationalist covers.

Our trips to the Back-Issue Store lasted for about a three-year period. While they may have enhanced my comic book fever, truth be told, we never really discovered any hidden treasures. Dreams of unearthing a mint-condition *Action Comics* #1 from 1938, which introduced the world to Superman, or the original *Detective Comics* #27 featuring "The Batman" never materialized. Like a lot of children of the '60s, we grew up hearing stories from our parents, who wistfully recalled owning all the classic superhero comics from the Golden Age of comic books during the late-Depression years. My father had a particular preference for Captain America and an aquatic hero with superhuman abilities named The Sub-Mariner (who had pointy ears, dark hair, wore a bathing suit, and resembled Leonard Nimoy's "Spock" in *Star Trek*), who would re-appear years later under the Marvel stable of superheroes.

It was a familiar story we would hear repeatedly from other children of our generation as well: by the time our parents had reached their teen years, they had lost all interest in comics; their parents, having seen no redeeming value in these childish possessions, had thrown out all of their comic book collections, along with their toys. Who could predict that, years later, these same items would become valuable collector's items in a burgeoning market for nostalgia?

Each time our parents told us this, we would be aghast, wondering how they lacked the foresight to save such obvious treasures, which would be worth a small fortune in our eyes. Rather than discouraging us, though, this only steeled our determination to seek rare comic books on our own. My father would also tell us about the Big Little Books that he collected as a child, including such titles as *Little Orphan Annie, Buck Rogers, Popeye, Mickey Mouse, Flash Gordon, Dick Tracy,* and *Captain Marvel.* He would lovingly describe their thick cardboard covers and the colorful artwork that would appear on each page opposite the text. Naturally, we added Big Little Books to our search for rare old comic books.

What we couldn't find at the Back-Issue Store· we sought elsewhere. Drew and I soon discovered a thrift shop not far from our home that had a bin by the front door filled with more current used comic books and magazines. The thrift's manager, a crafty old codger, would coyly tell us that he would occasionally spot an early

Action Comics or *Detective Comics,* but that we were always just a little too late. He cheerfully offered to sell us any rare valuable comics that we could find for the same price as any of the crappy comic books we typically found in the store: ten cents each.

"Even *Action Comics* #1?" I would ask incredulously, knowing its true soaring value thanks to Drew's copy of the latest *Comic Book Price Guide,* with visions dancing in my head of the first *Action Comics* cover showing the Man of Steel holding a green car in the air.

"Yup," he'd reply without any hesitation.

We thought we had pulled the wool over the old salesman's eyes. Unfortunately, we never discovered any valuable comics, despite the old man's entreaties to come back the next day, and we finally stopped returning after a number of disappointing visits.

Soon, my brothers and I would lose interest in the traditional superhero action comics genre altogether. But my search for comics would take an interesting twist. One evening in April of 1971, my parents dropped us off at the old Fillmore East concert hall on the Lower East Side. It was the first time I'd been left alone without my parents in the big city, and I remember feeling a sense of danger mixed with adventure.

We went to see a *Howdy Doody Show* revival featuring the red-haired, freckle-faced marionette and the affable '50s-era TV show's host, Buffalo Bob Smith. Before dropping us off, our parents issued stern warnings to my older brothers not to leave my side. Outside the Fillmore, a parade of hippies and street hawkers filled the teeming sidewalks.

Soon after being dropped off, ignoring our parents' warnings to stay put, my brothers promptly took me to a nearby magazine/head shop. And before I knew it we were looking at X-rated *underground comix* — avant-garde, uncensored, irreverent, and wildly obscene comics that originated in San Francisco and had made their way to Manhattan. This was my first exposure to comics drawn by an emerging generation of counterculture artists such as R. Crumb, Spain Rodriguez, S. Clay Wilson, Gilbert Shelton, and others who would defy all mainstream notions of what constituted a comic book.

Apparently, Josh had been quietly collecting these comics during his frequent forays into Manhattan with his friends to see rock concerts at the Fillmore East, enjoying such bands as the Allman Brothers, Mountain, Cactus, Chicago, Grand Funk Railroad, and a score of other seminal rock bands from the late '60s and early '70s. Drew and Josh were also secretly buying underground comix whenever we visited Bookmaster's, a trendy two-story mega-bookstore (now defunct) on the corner of Fifty-ninth and Third Avenue that also sold adult-themed counterculture books, records, and movie- and hippie-themed posters. (I still have my subversive Richard M. Nixon Coloring Book from 1969.)

Underground comix were so out there, however, that Josh and Drew wouldn't dare show them to our parents, who were perhaps the most liberal and tolerant of all the parents we had ever encountered. My brothers had collected comic books with such titles as *Zap*, *Bijou Funnies*, *Black and White*, *Hytone*, and *Yellow Dog*, each glorifying the hippie drug culture. The stories were satirical in nature, but were laced with explicit sexuality, were often misogynist, were chock full of profanities, contained scatological humor, and were blatantly racist.

Counterculture characters such as Fritz the Cat and Mr. Natural would soon become mainstream thanks to the growing popularity of R. Crumb's underground comix. The artwork was also unlike any comics we had ever seen before, the closest being *Mad* magazine; simply put, they were raw, sophomoric, sick, and, most importantly, often hilarious. Seeing these comics for the first time somehow set the stage for the *Howdy Doody Show* revival to follow.

Inside the Fillmore East, Buffalo Bob greeted the mostly long-haired audience, which had been weaned on the *Howdy Doody Show*. "Say kids, what time is it?" asked Buffalo Bob, decked out in his trademark red-fringed buckskin outfit, repeating the show's familiar opening refrain.

"It's Howdy Doody Time!" responded the appreciative, mostly stoned audience, which proceeded to sing the rest of the theme song in unison: *"It's Howdy Doody Time! It's Howdy Doody Time! ..."* Buffalo Bob asked how everyone was doing in the "Peanut Gallery," which led to another joyous response. A mushroom cloud of marijuana quickly filled the crowded theater like a ring of smog hovering over Los Angeles and I became dizzy from inhaling all the second-hand dope. In a nod to the changing times, Buffalo Bob would even crack a joke, feigning surprise in finding a pack of Zig Zag rolling papers, claiming it must have belonged to his old TV sidekick, Clarabell the Clown. The audience went wild.

Around this time, Drew had discovered the EC (Entertainment Comics) line of science fiction, suspense, and especially horror comic books from the 1950s. These included such classic titles as *Tales From the Crypt, The Vault of Horror,* and *The Haunt of Fear,* each featuring the familiar hosts — the Crypt-Keeper, the Vault-Keeper, and the Old Witch — drawn in small circles on the cover. Drew would relate to me how alarmed McCarthy-era '50s government agencies and school boards had sought to ban these graphic comics because of their disturbing depiction of gore and horrific violence, which, naturally, only served to heighten our interest.

Eventually a comic book code — not unlike the motion picture industry's film code from the '30s — was deployed by the comic book industry to censor itself from including content that was deemed too graphic in nature. Comic books that contained such words as "terror," "horror," and even "weird" in their titles were forbidden: rules clearly aimed at the EC line of comics and its iconoclastic founder, William Gaines, who had also launched *Mad* magazine around the same time.

Many of these horror comics that had been under fire folded by the mid-'50s, but now, a decade later, they were starting to resurface at comic book conventions, where they were considered valuable collector's items.

My brothers and I had an affinity for horror movies and monsters, so it was only natural that our interest would spill over into horror comic books as well. Since the late '60s, Drew and Josh had regularly purchased and sent away for issues of the horror comics magazines *Creepy* and *Eerie* from the advertisements in *Famous Monsters of Filmland*. I remember how excited they were when their magazines would arrive in the mail. My brothers even became official members of the Uncle Creepy Fan Club and Cousin Eerie Fan Club, each receiving honorary buttons drawn by the artist Jack Davis, plus an official membership diploma, which they proudly displayed in their rooms. I was too young to fully enjoy the story content of these magazines, but I was always impressed by the wonderful cover illustrations, especially those painted by the legendary fantasy comic book artist Frank Frazetta.

Unknowingly, we had had our first taste of EC comics when Josh had purchased a paperback in the mid-'60s called *Ray Bradbury's The Autumn People — Stories of Chilling Horror by the King of Fantasy*. I remember the haunting cover illustration, which showed zombie-like creatures rising from the ground beside an old tree under a misty harvest moon. The paperback was a reprint collection of Ray Bradbury stories that first appeared in the original 1950s EC horror and science fiction comics.

Soon after moving into Manhattan in 1972, Drew and I would begin attending comic book conventions held in Midtown hotels and convention centers. By now, Josh had lost all interest in comics, focusing instead on his guitar playing and writing. Armed with the latest *Comic Book Price Guide*, Drew and I would scour the convention halls looking for the best values, often meeting and obtaining autographs from some of Drew's comic book artist heroes. He would serve as my personal guide through this strange world of comic book collectors and dealers, steering me in the direction of the most innovative and interesting new and old-time illustrators, as well as those comics that would most likely become collector's items over time.

At first, most comic books looked pretty much the same to me, but I soon was able to discern what Drew dismissed as mere hacks — artists whose boring work would not stand the test of time — from the more talented illustrators. An artist like Frank Frazetta, for instance, was more like a classic painter, with an instantly recognizable style that was apparent even in his earliest work.

While I enjoyed reading comics, Drew was passionate about them. Not surprisingly, he would grow up to follow his childhood heroes by becoming an illustrator himself. Comic book illustrators were the equivalent of his sports stars, and he developed an encyclopedic knowledge of their statistics. Beyond the obvious artists who were household names, like Charles Schulz of *Peanuts*, he introduced me to such artist luminaries as Jack Kirby, Basil Wolverton, Bernie Wrightson, Will Eisner, Wally Wood, Harvey Kurtzman, Neal Adams, Jim Steranko, Jack Davis, "Ghastly" Graham Ingels, Al Feldstein, Joe Orlando, Johnny Craig, Reed Crandall, and Frank Frazetta. Why I still remember these names, nearly forty years after having last seen their actual work, is not only testament to the superior quality of their artwork but, more importantly, to Drew's influence on my interest in comic books.

I still have an autograph from the prolific comic book artist Al Williamson, including a quick illustration he made for me of Flash Gordon's arch nemesis Ming the Merciless. While Drew may have framed such items as important artifacts, I simply stored them on a pile with my comic books, quickly forgetting about them. For a time, Drew instructed me to buy #1s of all new DC and Marvel comics and to promptly seal them in air-tight plastic wraps because someday these premiere issues would be valuable to future collectors. Clearly, he wanted to avoid the same errors that our parents had made as children.

Based on his recommendations, I eagerly picked up the following #1s: *Conan the Barbarian*; *Swamp Thing*; *The Shadow*; *Kamandi, the Last Boy on Earth*; *Chilling Adventures in Sorcery*; and probably the most important purchase of all, the much-hyped *Shazam* ("The Original Captain Marvel"), which, Drew assured me, would someday be worth a small fortune. Perhaps my favorite purchase during this period was

The Demon #1, which was loosely based on the Arthurian legends of Camelot, beautifully drawn by Marvel Comics veteran Jack Kirby, who had caused a minor stir in comic book circles by jumping ship to DC Comics. I also picked up *Plop* #1, the "New Magazine of Weird Humor," featuring the freakishly delightful cover artwork of longtime *Mad* magazine contributor Basil Wolverton.

Along the way, I also started acquiring original EC horror comics from the '50s. None of these comics were in very good condition (they had a distinct old-paper smell, as if they had been left unattended for years in a box in someone's attic), and were probably unwise investments, but it was thrilling nonetheless to acquire the originals. Each time I removed a fragile copy from its protective plastic sheath, lifting the taped lip, I risked further damage to the comic. I would invariably chip a fading edge, undermining its value. But somehow that didn't bother me.

I once made the mistake, however, of purchasing for five dollars an original *Vault of Horror* #30 from 1953 (known as "the dismemberment cover") with the top third of the cover cleanly torn off. The remainder of the cover showed an arm severed down to the elbow socket still clenched to a subway overhead handrail while rush-hour passengers look on in abject horror and disgust. Drew was clearly upset — not by the shocking cover, beautifully illustrated by EC veteran Johnny Craig — but that I would be so stupid as to waste my money on a damaged comic that was basically worthless as an investment. He would bitterly complain to my father, who would later half-heartedly reprimand me, more so, I suspect, to placate Drew.

Disregard for taking good care of my comic books proved to be the eventual undoing of my comic book fever. Unlike Drew, who painstakingly sealed his comic books, lovingly protecting them from the elements and stocking them in order on neatly arranged bookshelves, even going so far as to catalogue his collection, I simply left my comics haphazardly in a pile. Drew would continue to attend comic book conventions, but he probably sensed my flagging interest and went without me.

Family moves led to further marginalization of my comic book collection. I was obviously more like my parents after all, quickly losing interest in comics as I grew up. Most of my comic books wound up stored in boxes, tucked away in closet spaces until I eventually sold them while in college, far below their *Comic Book Price Guide* market value, to comic book dealers who promptly inflated their price tags.

Looking back, it's hard to believe the grip comic book fever once held over my brother and me. I recently found a postcard that Drew had sent to me while I was attending Camp Emerson in Massachusetts during the summer of 1973. Throughout the summer, Drew had been sending me care packages filled with mostly comic books and I wrote him back at one point to thank him.

In my letter, I made mention of some of my favorite camp activities such as building model rockets. He wrote back: "Dear Mr. Flip [one of the pet names he used to call me], today is the 14th. You come here in around 10 days. On the 25th of August believe it or not there is a comic book convention in Amagansett at the American Legion Hall … You will probably get around 1 more package of comic books. Daaa!! I will just come out with it and say that the surprise you're getting is an E.C. comic. Don't expect no *Vault of Horror* #12. It ain't that old. You will see when you get here."

He had drawn two bizarre faces on the postcard: one of a portly, freckled man with neatly parted hair separated by a cowlick, wearing a tie, which was placed opposite the eight-cent stamp, and a smaller profile of an ugly woman with a bulbous nose and jutting chin within the text.

He ended the postcard, "P.S. Who cares about your stupid rockets?"

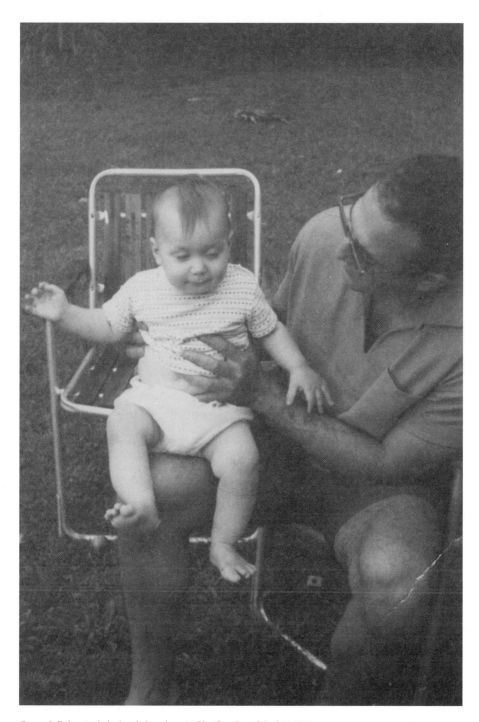

On my dad's knee in the backyard of our home in Glen Cove, Long Island, in 1961.

TOP: *Great, another boy—following two sons, my mother sorely wanted a daughter whom she hoped to name Gabby. Perhaps that's what accounts for my wide-eyed look of wonder?*

BOTTOM: *Always impeccably dressed, my grandfather Irving "Poppy" Friedman offers me some birthday cake in 1962. Sadly, the only thing I can remember him saying directly to me was, "Kipp-ah, would you like the pipik?"*

Calm before the storm--Sitting on a toy tractor with my oldest brother Josh in 1962. As we grew, our "playing" would be fraught with accidents, mishaps, and general roughhousing, plus many fun adventures.

Maternal grandfather Joseph "Papa" Howard teaches me to ride a bicycle on training wheels in 1962. Papa would later teach me to play chess, gin rummy and to always pour salt on cantaloupe and watermelon.

TOP: *Beside my perennially tanned paternal grandmother Molly "Nanny" Friedman in her Bronx apartment around 1964.*

BOTTOM: *At JFK Airport in 1965 awaiting our flight to the South of France where we would spend the summer. Pictured (left to right) are Irving "Poppy" Friedman, my father's fraternity brother Frank Borsky, (back row) Drew, me, Josh, and Bruce Jay, (sitting) our live-in babysitter Mrs. Isabelle Sullivan, Molly "Nanny" Friedman, and my mother, Ginger, with Piper, our Maltese cat.*

While visiting an antique shop in the French countryside in the summer of 1965, my mother thought it would be funny to sit me atop an oversized Louis XIV-era chair. I look more confused than amused.

Keep Out of My Kids' Hair—My brothers and I sporting Beatle haircuts (Josh, left; me, center; and Drew, right) along with our mother, Ginger, and Bruce Jay in a photo that accompanied my father's essay on the budding youth movement published in the Saturday Evening Post in 1966.

TOP: *With my childhood live-in babysitter Mrs. Isabelle Sullivan at our rented villa in the South of France during the summer of 1965. "I'm going to tell your fah-tha!" was a familiar admonishment of hers during our childhood.*

BOTTOM: *Brotherly love—My brothers and I in front of our house in Great Neck, Long Island in 1966. Drew plays with his Lambchop hand puppet over my head while Josh holds his guinea pig, Sweatie, in a blanket.*

Waiting to play catch with my father on the baseball fields at the Great Neck Estates Park in 1968.

TOP: *A family cruise aboard the S.S. Romantica over the Christmas-New Year's holiday in 1968. Family vacations were one of the bright spots in my parents' rocky marriage.*

BOTTOM: *My grandparents Poppy and Nanny looking stylish along the Bronx's Grand Concourse in the mid-1950s.*

My grandfather Papa beside his second wife, Sophie, in the mid-1960s. "Do you know why I like boys more than girls?" Sophie once asked my brothers and me. "Girls like diamonds."

Remember the Seventies?—Me (left) in front of our Great Neck house around 1971 with Josh (center) looking like one of his rock star heroes at the old Fillmore East concert hall alongside Drew holding the leash of our black Lab, Miranda.

TOP: *For the love of monsters--Drew looking maniacal while entering my room in a makeshift Dracula outfit, complete with fangs and a stuffed, torn Mickey Mouse t-shirt in 1972.*

BOTTOM: *Me in my Frankenstein's monster mask, menacingly holding a shoe for effect around 1972.*

TOP: *One of several comic book racks in Drew's unique room in Great Neck around 1972. Drew's walls were festooned with comic book art, MAD magazine covers and cutouts, Wacky Package bubblegum cards, baseball cards, monster movie pictures, B-movie posters, colorful hippie-era posters and popular advertisements.*

MIDDLE: *My autographed drawing of "Ming the Merciless" from the Flash Gordon cartoonist Al Williamson given to me at the 1974 New York Comic Con.*

BOTTOM: *A family shot taken on the terrace of my dad's Midtown Manhattan apartment around 1978. My dad gives me a hug while Josh (standing) and Drew (sitting), look on. Photo by Armen Katchaturian.*

From a high school yearbook photo shoot taken of me on the terrace of my dad's Manhattan apartment after I moved in with him in 1977 following my parents' divorce. Photo by Bruce Jay Friedman.

TOP: *My dad looking dapper on his 83th birthday in 2013. Photo by Kipp Friedman.*

BOTTOM: *Brunch with my dad at our favorite bagels & lox restaurant, Barney Greengrass, in 2012: Josh (left), me (center) and Drew (right). Photo by Barney Green grass, waiter.*

7. We've All Got Problems

Our babysitter, Mrs. Sullivan, once took me and my older brothers on an outing to the Morgan Memorial Park in Glen Cove, Long Island. It was named for the renowned financier J.P. Morgan, whose vast holdings included a sprawling estate along the shores of the Long Island Sound.

While playing on the park's band shell, my brother Josh suddenly grabbed me from behind by my ankles and started swinging me in a circle. He may have first asked me for my permission, but I can no longer remember. He was about age seven and more than four years older than I was, but we already had started roughhousing together (a trait that would continue through my early teens), so I would have happily agreed if asked. My arms flailed helplessly and I squealed with delight while the world streaked by in ever-increasing zigzagging lines. It felt exhilarating, like being on an amusement park twirling teapot ride, but I soon became dizzy and slightly nauseous, my squeals turning to low moans.

"Josh, put him down!" I heard Mrs. Sullivan's booming, high-pitched voice coming from just below the band shell, where she was passing the time smoking a Marlboro cigarette (her brand of choice) while my middle brother Drew swung happily on a nearby swing set. Ignoring her cries, Josh continued to spin me, even managing to increase the tempo of his revolutions. The world became one big blur.

"Josh, let him go! Let him go!" she shouted more insistently as she made her way toward the band shell. Mrs. Sullivan was a middle-aged woman with peroxide-blonde hair, and an imposing, heavy-set figure atop her squat five-foot frame.

"O-kay, Mrs. Sull-i-van!" my brother answered in a mischievous tone as Mrs. Sullivan reached him. He released his grip on my ankles, launching me from the band shell like a human shot put.

The sensation of suddenly floating in the air, with the cool breeze against my face, was even more exciting than being twirled by my ankles in circles, and for an instant I felt like my childhood TV cartoon hero *Gigantor,* the space-age robot, soaring through space. But my flight would be short-lived: I landed with a thud, face-first in a mound of sand alongside the swing set, chipping a baby tooth and cutting my upper lip. Dark blue and purple hues exploded like firecrackers before my eyes and my face went numb as I wiped mucus-coated sand from my mouth, my eyes starting to well up with tears.

I'm sure Mrs. Sullivan promptly reported the incident to my parents as soon as we returned home. "I'm going to tell your *fah-tha,*" was a familiar admonishment of hers during my childhood, typically delivered in her affected, East Coast-Brahmin accent tinged with hints of British aristocracy. (A third-generation Irish-American, Mrs. Sullivan had grown up in nearby Oyster Bay, Long Island.) And

Josh was most likely scolded by our parents. It wasn't the first time, nor would it be the last, but such are the travails of being the oldest brother.

As the youngest of three brothers, I typically avoided being left alone with Josh because it could be a recipe for disaster. It's not that my older brother had any ill intent; in most cases, he was simply bored and sought excitement (future psychologists would no doubt classify his behavior as ADHD), but the potential for danger was always there, and that is why Mrs. Sullivan was usually never far from my side. But she couldn't always be there.

Like the time when Josh took me sledding one snowy winter morning around the corner from our house on Robinson Avenue, a winding road connecting our hilltop neighborhood to the Glen Cove downtown shopping district. What better place, my eight-year-old brother reasoned, to go sledding, and who better to take than his little brother? I, of course, happily went along for the ride.

I'm sure our parents would have objected had they known, but they were probably still asleep, and Mrs. Sullivan had not yet moved in with us as our full-time babysitter and housekeeper. That left Josh in charge. I sat in front on a Radio Flyer sled with a firm grip on the sled's rope as we flew around the corner from our home and headed downhill, Josh using his longer legs to steer with his feet and avoid any cars that might pass alongside us.

About a quarter of the way down the hill we lost control and veered off course, slamming into a tree. If it weren't for my heavily padded red snowsuit that made me look like an overgrown maraschino cherry with legs poking out, I'm sure I would have sustained some injury instead of harmlessly slumping over. Josh, who was only wearing a light coat and a pair of jeans, absorbed the brunt of the collision, sustaining cuts and a badly bruised knee. Had we succeeded in completing our ride, though, our path would have taken us directly into the teeth of downtown traffic. I'm sure Josh was once again reprimanded for his recklessness.

"We've all got problems." It's something a more mature Josh would explain to me years later, adopting a professorial tone as if addressing a student. "I've got problems and so do *you*," he noted, pointing a bony, cigarette-stained finger at me for emphasis. It was a revelation he had learned after starting to see his psychiatrist, Dr. Friend, and he was eager to impart his newfound wisdom after another of our verbal spats, which seemed to be occurring with more regularity.

At age ten, I didn't think I had any problems — other than sometimes bothersome older brothers — but I resented Josh lumping me in with what I felt were his very real problems. "Yeah, *you're* my problem!" I quickly responded in my excited, prepubescent voice. Then he made what was perhaps the single most annoying gesture that I can recall in all my childhood years: he raised his index finger to his mouth and issued a brief "Shhhh!" sound as though snuffing out a match.

More effective than any punch he could have thrown or anything he could have yelled, I felt like I was being summarily dismissed by an overlord, which, quite naturally, only raised my ire. Noticing my exasperation, he repeated the offending gesture, infuriating me anew, but effectively shutting me up.

At age fifteen, Josh stood nearly six feet tall with wavy chestnut-brown hair that fell below his pointy shoulders. He was once a promising Little League pitcher with a wicked fastball until he threw out his arm, effectively ending his pitching career before it even got started. He now focused most of his energies on playing the guitar, making great strides after taking lessons from jazz guitar legend Jim Hall, who also lived in Great Neck.

Josh looked like one of the pale, rail-thin musicians on the posters that were plastered on his wall from some of his favorite late '60s rock bands like *Cactus, The Jimi Hendrix Experience,* and *Mountain.* He was underweight for his V-shaped frame and he had a recurring case of acne. More disturbingly, he had developed a nervous habit of gnawing on his knuckles, which were sometimes bloody and raw.

I was vaguely aware of the ongoing difficulties he was experiencing with his teachers and the administration at Great Neck South High School, often being singled out for the smallest infraction. It got so bad that one day a teacher called my mother to report he was spotted eating pretzels in the hallway. My mother chewed out the stunned teacher for worrying her unnecessarily, telling her she should be thankful that Josh was safe and sound when many students were found on campus overdosing on drugs.

I was aware that Josh was having problems at home as well, my parents having banned certain boys from our house because they were "bad influences" on Josh, but I never saw Josh actually do drugs. I had my suspicions though, especially when I caught him burying a package in the front yard one evening and he made me promise not to tell my parents.

Once highly alert, athletic, and outgoing, Josh now seemed noticeably changed, and it sometimes felt like I was living with a complete stranger. Often distant and lethargic, he would occasionally nod off, bleary-eyed, at the breakfast table. He was also subject to occasional mood swings, behaving erratically and disagreeably when I least expected it. Due to my more confrontational nature, I'm sure I was not totally innocent in our interactions, and I would occasionally egg him on as younger siblings are wont to do.

He had a loping, camel-like gait, for instance, that Drew and I enjoyed parodying. Then there was his gasping, helium-high laugh that sounded more like a cry — ""Heh! Heh! Heh! Heh! Heh!" — that reminded me of his guinea pig Sweetie's squeaks. I probably imitated his laugh on occasion, too, just out of earshot.

Drew and I mostly ignored Josh's mood swings, although I remember once getting into a heated altercation at the breakfast table after Josh had made disparaging remarks about Mrs. Sullivan's cooking. I grabbed a handful of spaghetti and meatballs from my plate and flung it at Josh, splattering red sauce across his face, which was partially concealed behind a mop of stringy hair.

Enraged, he scooped up a handful of spaghetti and fired it back and then we both stood, yelling at each other. Red sauce was everywhere. It must have looked like a scene from a horror movie to my brother Drew, who watched in disbelief. Just as blows were about to be exchanged, Mrs. Sullivan came in and hoisted a wicker chair, poking the legs at Josh like a muumuu-wearing lion tamer while he swung wildly at her.

After some tense moments, order was restored without any blows having been landed and Josh's anger lifted. He suddenly became jovial and started chanting, mockingly, with a big grin, "SULLIVAN! SULLIVAN! SULLIVAN! SULLIVAN! SULLIVANNNN!" We had recently seen the long-running Off-Broadway hit musical *The*

Fantasticks at the Sullivan Street Playhouse in Greenwich Village. Mrs. Sullivan harrumphed and shook her head in disbelief as she made her way back to the kitchen.

As the youngest of three fairly active boys, each two years apart in age, I've certainly experienced my share of normal teasing, fights, and sibling rivalry over the years. But despite our differences, I never doubted that we all cared about each other, and would even come to each other's defense, if necessary. It's just that I cannot recall ever expressing even the faintest amount of actual affection toward each other throughout my childhood. Sure, we tolerated each other — sort of like cats living under the same roof. Forget brotherly love, though; ours was more like brotherly indifference. At some point I thought that older brothers were supposed to represent this mythic source of guidance and inspiration for younger siblings. But early on, I quickly came to the realization that this was not to be the case in our household.

How different we were from our parents' and grandparents' generation, where siblings would regularly give each other great big bear hugs and plant kisses on each other's cheeks and lips, a trait no doubt that carried over from our family's Eastern European Jewish origins. Family legend has it that my maternal grandfather, Papa, and his four older brothers once threw a member of an Irish gang off a rooftop after experiencing an anti-Semitic incident in Harlem in the early 1920s. Early photos capture our awkwardness, as it appears almost painful for my brothers and me to stand next to each other, usually at our mother's behest.

Our mutual indifference may stem from the fact that all three of us were so different. Josh was restless, extroverted, had a unique talent for getting into mischief and, at the same time, was very creative and highly sensitive to criticism. My mother claims that he might have hit his head after she accidentally dropped him off the changing table when he was an infant. Because of his seriousness and intensity, plus his proclivity for wearing a doctor's gown and stethoscope as a child, Mrs. Sullivan would dub him early on "The Professor."

Drew was quieter, less confrontational, particularly focused — especially when doodling in little sketchbooks — and blessed with a natural ability to imitate people's voices and mannerisms (characteristics that would serve him well as a successful illustrator later in life). I was probably a mixture of both my brothers, with big, round hazel-colored eyes that seemed to soak in everything going on around me. Indeed, my eyes were often the first thing people noticed about me. Many early photos show my moon-faced bald head staring back in wide-eyed astonishment, as if marveling at the world around me, while my brothers would typically mug for the camera. One intergenerational photo, taken moments before boarding a plane for a family trip to France in the summer of 1965, shows my brothers mimicking the blank, wide-eyed stares of the evil, fair-haired Hitler-youth-like children in the movie *The Village of the Damned*. I wasn't in on the joke and instead smiled broadly for the camera.

My childhood memories with my brothers can be characterized as a series of mishaps and irresponsibility, combined with endless teasing and many shared fun adventures. Despite occasional bumps and bruises along the way, in retrospect it's amazing we survived intact without sustaining any major injuries. There certainly were a number of close calls. Like the time we went bodysurfing in the Atlantic Ocean in East Hampton one gray, blustery summer morning in the early '70s following a hurricane. The ocean was unusually choppy as white-capped waves crested like laundry detergent in a washing machine, crashing at multiple points along the shoreline.

Despite my pleas, my brothers had enough sense to insist that I not enter the surf with them. Instead, I would wait with our black Lab, Miranda, on a deserted stretch of beach by a life preserver attached to a pole just in case they got into trouble. There was probably little I could do; they swam out further into the surf than I could have possibly flung the life preserver. After watching their futile attempts at bodysurfing, I could tell something was wrong, as they seemed to struggle just to remain afloat, their heads occasionally disappearing beneath the surf.

Finally, they made it back to shore, each relating how there were hairy moments when each thought the strong undertow would sweep them out to sea. All I could think of was: what would I tell my parents?

Reckless? True. But not any more reckless, I suppose, than the time my brothers placed a thin rope around my waist when I was about eight and coaxed me to climb out from a third-story window of our home so that I could walk on the roof. Josh once told me that when he was about seven he had climbed through the railing and almost fallen off the top of the Empire State Building, although I thought he was exaggerating, probably imagining himself at the time as King Kong being shot at by war planes. But then, he used to exaggerate a lot. I believed it, for instance, when he told me that there was one particular strand of hair on your head that if you plucked it your brains would seep out. For an entire week, I avoided combing my hair, fearful of accidentally dislodging that one hair follicle that might empty out my brains.

My earliest memory of my brothers is of them bouncing up and down joyfully on a trampoline one sunny spring day. I was about two years old and was watching them through a window from my crib in the first-floor utility room off the kitchen. I must have been attracted to the motion and sound of their playing, and I knew instinctively that I wanted to participate.

I remember how the three of us enjoyed piling on top of our father in our backyard at night after he returned from his job editing men's adventure magazines in Manhattan. Being the youngest, I would wrap myself safely around my father's ankles while my brothers flung themselves at his massive arms, neck, and upper torso while he swatted at them like gnats. It was a game we had created, played mostly in slow motion, with our father as Hercules from the low-budget, poorly dubbed Italian movies starring former bodybuilder Steve Reeves that we enjoyed watching on TV. Afterward, we would tear off chunks from crusty loaves of Italian bread and greedily stuff our mouths, making exaggerated grunting noises imitating how we imagined Hercules and his hungry Greek Argonaut companions ate after victorious combat.

During the early 1960s, Josh began buying issues of *Famous Monsters of Filmland* magazine from Vic's, a magazine and candy store in downtown Glen Cove, quickly amassing a sizeable collection of original issues, which he kept in a neat stack in his bedroom. These were his prized possessions. As is often the case with sibling rivalries, at some point Drew could no longer contain his desire for these magazines. He had already developed a habit of playing with and breaking many of Josh's toys.

So when one day Josh walked in and found Drew tearing out pictures from his monster magazines all hell broke loose, and Josh would once again be reprimanded for his actions. From that point on, though, he would lock his door to prevent any further damage. I would soon move into Drew's room next to Josh's on the second floor and to pass the time, Drew and I would occasionally play in the hallway outside Josh's locked door, squealing and making other childish noises to get our older brother's attention. His yells at us to be quiet were all the motivation we needed to continue.

One day one of us had the idea of sliding our fingers under Josh's door while he was at his desk trying to do his homework. Since my hands were smaller, Drew helped push the soles of my feet so I could get better leverage, allowing me to wiggle my fingers, like a cat's paw, under the door. We were both laughing hysterically when I heard Josh's hurried footsteps as he got up, approached the door, and in one swift motion opened and then slammed it shut.

A rush of air brushed against my face followed by what felt like an electric jolt passing through my arm. When I looked down I noticed the top of my left middle finger hanging off the bone. As blood started to pool, I started screaming and went into shock. (Clearly, it was an accident, but I suspect my mother has yet to truly forgive Josh.)

My father rushed me to the nearby North Shore Hospital, and I remember riding in the front seat of his white Buick with a kitchen towel and icepack wrapped around my throbbing hand. My mother and older brothers must have followed separately. My father had a steely look on his face as he drove, occasionally glancing over at me, offering words of encouragement while I whimpered, still in shock.

The attending physician in the emergency wing that day was named Dr. Bang, an irony not lost on my brothers and me. I watched with a sense of detachment and awe, between occasional sniffles, as Dr. Bang calmly applied thirteen stitches to the top digit of my middle finger as though sewing buttons on a shirt. Afterward, he bandaged up my hand, which now resembled one of Hercules's battering clubs. (When the bandages finally came off a week later, the crescent-shaped stitches reminded me of the erratic surgical marks across the Frankenstein monster's head where his brains had been removed. I enjoyed showing off the jagged, raw-looking stitches to my brothers and friends for its shock value as well as a sort of badge of honor.)

Adjacent to the waiting room was a vending machine stocked with useful items for extended hospital stays, including cheap plastic children's toys. When I re-joined my mother and brothers in the waiting room, my brothers presented me with a miniature toy skeleton that they had purchased from the vending machine. They called him Mr. Bones and I believed it when they told me how Mr. Bones had stood on Dr. Bang's shoulders like Jiminy Cricket in *Pinocchio*, whispering helpful instructions into his ear while my finger was being stitched and bandaged. It felt comforting to know that Mr. Bones and Dr. Bang were in my corner.

The teasing began in earnest after we had moved from Glen Cove to Great Neck in the summer of 1966 so that we could be closer to Manhattan. I'm not sure what precipitated the teasing, but most of it was your garden-variety sibling behavior. For instance, there was a girl I liked named Lisa who lived across the street whom I had secretly played doctor with in first grade. Drew would occasionally call out, "Lisa [G's] coming up the stairs!" while I was still in bed watching TV. I always fell for that one, tripping over myself as I hurriedly pulled up my trousers, never once questioning why she would be in our house to visit me on an early Saturday morning while I was still in my underwear.

Drew would soon come up with nonsensical, made-up words to irritate me. One particular word he repeated often was "klaintz." We'd be at a restaurant and he would first check to see that no one was looking and then whisper, "Klaintz." Before I knew it, I would howl in disapproval and my mother would tell me to quiet down, while Drew looking on innocently with a "Who me?" expression. Naturally, just when things settled down, he'd fire over another "klaintz" like a missile just under the radar. "He said it again!" I would shout.

Another favorite word of his, inexplicably, was "sauce," which he would repeat with the same results. It got to the point where all he had to do was simply stare at me and I'd yell, "He's lookin' at me!" Drew knew just how far to push my buttons, usually stopping at the point when I would shout: "Goddamnit!" — the worst word I knew at the time.

Another bone of contention was the all-important bedtime hour. Drew and I slept in separate bedrooms across the hall from one another, but I could see his light still on from the reflection cast in my window when I was certain we had the same bedtime. My complaints about this seeming injustice, however, fell on deaf ears and Drew would lord over this inequity, just as he had years prior when we shared a bedroom, divided by a thick line of chalk, and he would step over my side of the room to get to the door.

Sometime in third grade, my mother had had enough of my constant whining about my brother's teasing and decided to send me to a child psychiatrist named Dr. Cove, a mild-mannered blonde woman who reminded me of TV psychiatrist and columnist Dr. Joyce Brothers. Of course, Mrs. Sullivan was given the task of driving me after school in her old mustard yellow station wagon with faux wood paneling to Dr. Cove's office, which was located in a red brick office building across the street from Clover Drive Elementary School. Mrs. Sullivan would drive me home and shake her jowly, bulldog-like freckled face in disapproval while puffing on a Marlboro cigarette, reassuring me that there was nothing wrong with me.

Despite her assurances, I remember feeling self-conscious about seeing a psychiatrist and kept this secret from even my closest friends. It made me think of a classmate of mine named Freddy, who was having difficulty coping with his parents' recent divorce. I was also vaguely aware of the negative connotation of the word "shrink," having heard the term used derogatively by my parents. Added to which, our home was literally hemmed in on all sides by practicing psychiatrists (who, incidentally, were some of the worst candy-givers at Halloween). There was old Dr. Katz and his wife, who lived like hermits, to our immediate left (they handed out stale, bitter black licorice dots) and the always taciturn, stern-looking Dr. Schanberg on our right, whose three sons I occasionally clashed with over the years. Several other psychiatrists also lived across the street and down the block. Indeed, our block on Gateway Drive in the Village of Great Neck Estates may very well have been, at the time, the psychiatrist capital of Long Island.

My sessions with Dr. Cove lasted for about two months. I usually sat with legs crossed on a colorful carpet in her dimly lit office playing *Candyland*, *Chutes & Ladders*, and *Hi Ho! Cherry-O* while she asked me probing questions in a calm voice, taking copious notes in a yellow pad. I mostly talked about my brother's teasing and the normal pitfalls of being the youngest brother, territory she had undoubtedly covered with dozens of other children many times before. She may have offered useful advice, but mostly I remember her just listening and nodding reassuringly. I don't think I had ever met anyone so placid in my life.

After my final session with Dr. Cove, Mrs. Sullivan greeted me in the waiting room and once again assured me in her exasperated voice reminiscent of British royalty, "There's absolutely *nothing* wrong with you. Your *muh-tha's* the crazy one."

I guess it could have been worse. My parents had progressive friends who raised their daughter for the first two years of her life in a "Skinner Box," named after the renowned behavioral psychologist B.F. Skinner, who had advocated placing toddlers in a special protective aquarium-like container. I remember the disoriented toddler tumbling down our stairwell like a Slinky whenever visiting our house. (The daughter would grow up to be a renowned businesswomen in her high-profile profession, perhaps validating the effectiveness of the "Skinner Box.")

The Dr. Cove sessions ended abruptly without any resolution, although my mother would insist years later that they were indeed beneficial. I would respond, sarcastically, that we must have reached a breakthrough somewhere between *Hi Ho! Cherry-O* and *Candyland*. Apparently, my mother felt that my brother Drew was having problems of his own and decided to send him to his one and only therapy session with Josh's psychiatrist, Dr. Friend.

Drew was becoming inattentive at school, occasionally climbing out of classroom windows at Great Neck South while his teachers weren't looking. He also had a habit of drawing pictures on desks of his teachers' exaggerated, but anatomically correct, private parts. Recognizing his proclivity for drawing, my mother once took Drew to the Metropolitan Museum of Art in Manhattan to expose him to some of the art world's masterpieces. Drew held his head down defiantly and sulked throughout the entire visit, refusing to look at any of the great works of art. In his worldview, the only true art masterpieces could be found within the pages of *Mad* magazine.

Drew's session with Dr. Friend would also have inconclusive results: my brother and the good doctor stared at each other in silence for the entire hour, locked in a sort of Mexican standoff, each waiting for the other to say something. Afterward, my mother reasoned — correctly — that any future therapy would be just as fruitless.

I'm not so sure my sessions with Dr. Cove were that helpful either, other than serving as a good outlet for me to express myself. At the time, only Dr. Cove and Mrs. Sullivan truly knew how I felt. One unexpected outcome of my sessions, however, was that I would start to blame myself for my parents' frequent squabbles. Like a lot of children caught in the middle of their parents' marital difficulties, I had reached the conclusion that my fighting with my brothers was causing an ever-widening rift between my parents, so I made a conscious effort to curb my complaining, thinking they would draw closer together. This, of course, didn't work.

Seemingly overnight, it appeared that the majority of my parents' friends were either divorced or separated. Even many of my closest friends' parents were having marital problems. I would sometimes accompany my best friend Bruce Altman on weekend outings when his father had visitation rights, and I would get to know his "Uncle Buddy" who lived in his house. It seemed as though an epidemic of divorce and marital re-alignment had broken out all around us and was slowly encroaching on our home.

I remember one day my mother's friend Eileen visited us with her new boyfriend, an Australian named Roger whom she had recently met at a singles' bar in Midtown Manhattan. Eileen was divorced from her husband of twenty-plus years with whom she had raised several grown children. She was now head-over-heels in love with Roger, the two of them already happily plotting their new life together. My mother was especially happy for her friend's good fortune. Short, muscular, and gregarious, Roger had a thick Aussie accent and said he was a member of the Australian Olympic diving team. He was also probably the hairiest person I had ever met in my life, his face buried beneath a mound of black Outback brush. Within days, a distraught Eileen would return in tears to relate how Roger — if that even was his name — was a con man with a wife and children back home in Australia who had disappeared shortly after she had lent him several thousand dollars.

Each of us reacted differently to our parents' attempts to patch up their marital problems. While Drew never missed an opportunity to continue to tease me, it was always good natured and, being the youngest, I secretly enjoyed the attention. He quickly lost interest in most subjects at school, focusing instead on his guinea pig Squeaky, comic books, his budding artwork, and watching endless hours of cartoons, classic movies, and old sitcoms on TV.

Josh developed a bit of a bullying streak, taking out his frustrations on younger kids in the neighborhood. He enjoyed pinning younger boys down on the ground and demanding that they recite statements like: "You're the king, Josh" and "I worship you, Josh."

One day he did this to my best friend Bruce Altman. A few days later, while Bruce and I played basketball in our backyard, Josh came out and started to scold Bruce for stripping shingles from our garage roof and flinging them like Frisbees across the backyard. In truth, it was my idea to peel and fling the shingles — something my father had already had a talk with me about — but Josh chose to single out my friend anyway.

I felt like something snapped inside. Momentarily seeing red, I swung my right arm sideways with all my might, landing a sucker punch like a Heimlich maneuver into the pit of Josh's stomach. He collapsed in a heap, all the wind knocked out of him. His face turned beet red as he writhed on hands and knees for over a minute, at one point extending an arm upward as though he were trying to tell me something, but the words would not come out.

Bruce looked on in confusion and I stared down at Josh, who was slowly starting to recover his breath, and just when I could finally understand what he was trying to say, I took off running. He finally caught up with me in the backyard of a friend's house down the block. A small crowd of neighbors had gathered around us, attracted by the commotion from Josh's shouts as he chased me through the neighborhood. He attempted to pin my arm behind my back so he could replicate the punch to my stomach but I proved too elusive and he soon gave up after a few failed swings. After that incident, however, his bullying streak ended.

At some point, my parents decided that a change of scenery was what they needed to shore up their marriage. My brothers were clearly not flourishing at Great Neck South High School, despite its reputation for academic excellence, and they didn't think I would fare well there either. Something pivotal but secretive had also happened to Josh, who was noticeably more alert and no longer behaving as erratically as before, and it seemed that my parents had taken a renewed interest in him. Still, it became obvious that my parents were going in separate directions. There was talk of packing up the family and moving to Italy, where my brothers and I would attend an American school in Rome, but that was just idle chatter.

My father had maintained an apartment in Midtown Manhattan, where he was spending more time during the week, and my mother was often out and about with her girlfriends in Manhattan. The only constant in my life was Mrs. Sullivan.

Despite our occasional differences, Josh and I would stop fighting and even grow closer, mostly through music. He had been taking guitar lessons for years and I had started to play the violin in school. For several years he had been attending rock concerts at the old Fillmore East concert hall on the Lower East Side until its eventual demise in 1971.

When my father bought me a record player for my eleventh birthday, Josh accompanied me to a local record store, making musical recommendations. When I bought my first album, by The Jackson Five, he suggested that I also buy Jimi Hendrix's *Band of Gypsys* album recorded live from the Fillmore East. I shelved that album after just one listen, preferring The Jackson Five, but years later would grow to fully appreciate Josh's recommendation.

When we finally left Great Neck for a new beginning in Manhattan in the spring of 1972, little did we know that that would be the last time we would remain as a nuclear family. Josh's revelation that "We've all got problems" would ultimately prove true, serving as the greatest lesson a big brother could ever give a younger brother.

8. Breaking Up Is Hard to Do

The first time I saw a woman naked was in late 1970 while attending the final performance of my father's Off-Broadway play *Steambath* at the Truck and Warehouse Theatre on the Lower East Side of Manhattan.

I was ten and my father thought it important that I see his satirical play depicting the afterlife as a steambath and God as a Puerto Rican attendant — despite its brief nudity and use of profanity — before it closed. My attention, however, was somewhat distracted by my older brothers' glowing accounts of the play's nude shower scene, so when an attractive blonde actress strolled across the stage, nonchalantly disrobed, and quickly showered — making a gleeful squeal as the water splashed across her body — I should have felt more excitement. Instead, it happened so suddenly and matter-of-factly that I felt more like a voyeur self-consciously peeping through a keyhole.

We left the theater into an awaiting limo, and as we drove off, my father asked the driver to stop momentarily. In hopped the pretty actress whom I had earlier seen naked. She was dressed in what appeared to be the same white terrycloth bathrobe that she'd worn in the play. As she took a seat next to us, I could detect the scent of herbal shampoo in her hair and feel the warmth her body still radiated as if she had just stepped out of a shower. In my giddiness, I hardly noticed my mother's absence.

I'm not sure when it first dawned on me that my parents were having marriage problems. Growing up, I heard the story about a party my parents held at a rented beach house while we were staying on Fire Island during the summer in 1963. With the alcohol flowing, my father left the party with an attractive blonde woman. Suspecting something was awry, my mother followed them onto the deck where she promptly found them, grabbed a sprinkler hose, and watered them down.

The blonde woman screamed, "I'm a lesbian! I'm a lesbian! I don't even like men!" while my mother's friend, Gerri David, shouted, "Oy Vey!" Dripping wet, my father began laughing and the blonde woman ran off. My parents weathered that storm, and it even became a source of humor, but apparently there were other forces at work that would put greater strain on their marriage.

Maybe because I was the youngest and less observant than my older brothers, it never occurred to me that anything was out of the ordinary in my parents' marriage. Indeed, I knew a number of classmates whose parents were separated or divorced, so I reasoned that my parents' still-intact marriage was somehow stable and secure. Looking back, though, as pleasant and magical as my memories were of a childhood as the son of a successful writer and an equally creative mother, there were a number of early warning signs of trouble brewing ahead.

One of my earliest memories that all was not as it appeared occurred in 1968, when I was about seven. I had just returned home from school when my mother introduced me to a man named Marc M., who spoke with a German accent but was Swiss. He was handsome, in a Maximilian Schell sort of way, with dark wavy hair, and he had an old world, courtly charm. My father was away on business at the time.

Marc was visiting, ostensibly, to view my mother's exhibit of Plexiglas art and jewelry creations that she kept stored in a large pantry room off the kitchen area of our home in Great Neck, New York. She was preparing for a showcase of her work at a Manhattan gallery, and the room was teeming with odd-shaped bits of multi-colored futuristic Plexiglas creations. Items scattered around the room included oversized rings, necklaces, bracelets, end tables, ash trays, and decorative cubes — as well as sheets of bubble wrap, which I enjoyed popping.

The only reason I recall this chance encounter back in 1968 is because that day I had peed my pants on the long walk home from Clover Drive Elementary School. My white corduroys were wet and clingy and I could feel a rash forming on my inner thighs. With moist fingers, I sheepishly shook Marc's hand. I could sense from his nervous smile that this was an awkward moment for him as well, only for different reasons.

Our housekeeper, Mrs. Sullivan, tended to my wet corduroys and it was clear to me that she was not pleased by Marc's presence. She came up with a nickname for Marc — "Nazi Monkey" — which she would utter a bit too loudly.

Marc, I would later learn, was a lounge singer whom my mother had met during the summer of 1967 at a restaurant where he was performing in Bridgehampton, Long Island. We were staying at a rented beach house in nearby Amagansett. During that fabled "Summer of Love," I memorized all the songs on the Beatles' latest LP, *Sgt. Pepper's Lonely Hearts Club Band*. My father's friend, the writer Terry Southern, who was staying with his family in a beach house not far from ours, had given us a copy. His picture is on that celebrated cover. (He's standing in front of Lenny Bruce and next to Dylan Thomas and the singer Dion.) I was too busy singing "When I'm Sixty-Four" with Mrs. Sullivan to notice that my mother had begun a relationship with another man.

Most of the summer, my father remained in Manhattan, working on the production of his play *Scuba Duba*, — ironically, a tense comedy about a New York couple vacationing in the south of France when the wife decides to run off with a black scuba diver.

A few years later, while I was at sleep-away camp, Marc and my mother would run off together — at least for the summer. Almost daily, I would receive picture postcards as they traveled throughout Europe. The postcards first arrived from Switzerland, where she was staying with Marc's family. They showed idyllic images of the famous Alps, bars of Swiss chocolate, Swiss cheese, and lots of dairy cows. Soon I would receive a flurry of postcards from Austria and Germany, depicting medieval castles with moats, and then more castles and country scenes from Spain and Portugal.

I would also receive occasional letters from my father, who was on the road with his latest play, *Turtlenecks*, starring Tony Curtis, which was having out-of-town runs along the East Coast. My father was consumed with anxious hopes that his play would make it to Broadway. (It closed out-of-town.) I remember he wrote optimistically of how Sammy Davis had loved one performance. Despite my parents' separate paths that summer, it still seemed all was business as usual, and I assumed our family would be back together when I returned from summer camp.

And my parents did return by the end of the summer, only I would soon discover that my mother had replaced their king-sized bed with matching antique twin brass beds. Although the beds were spaced only a few feet apart, to me they represented a bigger gulf than the geographic distances that separated my parents the previous summer. Their bedroom had always been a refuge of sorts, where my brothers and I spent evenings watching family movies like *The Wizard of Oz* and *It's a Wonderful Life* on their TV. With the arrival of the twin beds, I remember feeling confused as to where to sit, thinking I would be showing disloyalty by choosing one bed over the other; instinctively, my brothers and I would soon retreat to our own rooms to watch TV.

Unbeknownst to me, my father had begun renting an apartment on the thirtieth floor of the ultra-modern Phoenix high-rise building on East Sixty-fifth Street and Third Avenue in Manhattan. He would call it his "tower of steel and glass." This is where he holed up during his increasingly frequent overnight stays. Somehow I failed to connect the dots and saw his absences as nothing more than his occasional business trips to Hollywood, where he would work on screenplays.

Despite several trial separations, my parents made a number of valiant attempts at reconciliation, although I'm not sure if they ever went to the extent of actually seeking marriage counseling. One such memory of this period sticks in my mind: my parents were sitting happily together on an overstuffed chair one summer morning in East Hampton. My mother was in her nightgown, with my father joking that this was their "third" attempt at reconciliation. They were laughing, even flirting with each other, and all seemed so natural to me; in retrospect, it was probably the last time I saw them so happy together.

By 1972, my mother would become more open with me and my brothers on how they were seeking ways to save their marriage, which had a ring of optimism — like saving the whales — at one point even raising the notion of moving the family to Italy, far from the distracting New York influences that she thought were pulling them apart. I think my father mostly indulged her ideas, but when push came to shove, we sold our house in Great Neck and moved into Manhattan. Just prior to our move, my mother held an estate sale and a line of neighbors and antique dealers queued outside our home one bright Saturday morning. I remember neighbors squabbling over our family's possessions; it was as if vultures had descended upon our living room, picking apart a carcass.

My parents' final attempt to stay together coincided with a mostly dispirited family vacation to Puerto Rico in early 1972. We stayed at the San Juan Hilton, visited brown-sanded beaches dotted with palm trees, and explored much of the verdant countryside as well as the capital city of San Juan.

One night, we visited a restaurant in downtown San Juan recommended to us by my father's friend, Mario Puzo, because of its reputation for wonderful paella. The restaurant was located in a Spanish Colonial-era home with a huge tree growing in the middle of the dining room. Upon leaving the restaurant, my father amusingly pointed out all the transvestites prowling the streets. They looked like heavily rouged stevedores and cab drivers in poorly fitted wigs and loud, patterned dresses.

Unlike on previous family vacations, my parents' steady bickering, followed by long silences, became more obvious to us boys and we could see them splitting apart before our eyes.

While visiting a rain forest, a guide pointed out a peculiar plant that shriveled and shied away from human contact called the "touch-me-not" plant. This strange plant seemed to embody the fragile state of my parents' marriage.

When we moved into Manhattan, I first stayed with my father in his apartment at the Phoenix for a few days while my mother and my older brothers prepared for the move into our apartment at the El Dorado twin tower high-rise building on Central Park West and Ninetieth Street. My father's apartment at the Phoenix offered a dizzying panorama of Midtown Manhattan, especially at night, when the city seemed to light up like a million candles.

He decorated the apartment sparingly with dark leather couches, contemporary track lighting, and unfamiliar furniture and dinnerware, but I did recognize one item: an abstract painting made of overlaying white strips of plaster that my mother had purchased at an art gallery in East Hampton the previous summer. The piece reminded me of a body cast that had completely splintered apart, with the plaster dripping white dust whenever it was touched. I remember how messy it was, clinging to your clothes as you passed. He soon discarded it.

After a few days of my father and I living like bachelors, I rejoined my mother and brothers at the El Dorado across town. My father, however, remained at the Phoenix, choosing instead to visit us for dinner on weekends and then leave. It was as if my parents were now dating, and my mother wanted to make sure he had a nice homemade meal (prepared by our housekeeper, Mrs. Sullivan, of course). After dinner, my father would relax in our apartment's living room and library, where he would smoke his Macanudo cigars and sip cognac while reading or listening to records. The next morning, the room would still smell of his cigars, and sometimes I would relight the butts I found in ashtrays and turn green after a few ill-advised puffs.

My father soon stopped visiting us at our apartment altogether, and within a few months, my mother would announce that there would be "some changes" and "belt-tightening." The only change I noticed at first was that she had purchased about a dozen loaves of rye bread that quickly grew stale — her futile attempt at economizing.

She did, however, begin actively seeing other men. Mrs. Sullivan would pass judgment on her dates. David was a clean-cut, well-dressed businessman who Mrs. Sullivan thought was marriage material for my mother, but whom my mother found "too boring." Mrs. Sullivan was clearly unimpressed with Steve, a long-haired acting student who rode a motorcycle and who was a Vietnam vet. Then there was a man whose name escapes me who looked to be no older than my oldest brother Josh, then about eighteen. In an attempt to win favor with me, this latest suitor would tell me all about his belief in out-of-body experiences.

One day while my mother was talking with Steve on the phone in the kitchen, my brother Drew walked in and my mother, knowing Steve was an acting student, announced: "Oh, Drew just walked in! He does wonderful imitations. Would you like to hear one?" She handed Drew the phone and walked out of the kitchen briefly.

Seizing the opportunity, Drew launched into a pitch-perfect Edward G. Robinson: "Listen, you! ... Do you know how old my mother is ... See?" When my mother returned, he handed her the phone. Steve must have been in shock and said something that disturbed her because my mother screamed into the phone: "What did Drew say to you? What did he say? Oh my God!"

Drew walked out of the kitchen with a look of satisfaction and that was the last we ever heard from Steve the actor.

Occasionally, Marc M. would reappear, like a long-lost uncle, with Mrs. Sullivan reprising the "Nazi Monkey" nickname she had given him years ago. Once, Marc and my mother even attempted to set up her slightly overweight girlfriend, Karen, on a double date with Marc's friend, Helmut. When Helmut finally met Karen, he backed away from her in a panic, sweeping his hands defensively and stuttering in broken English, "No! No! Please! Please!" before making a hasty retreat.

My father also began dating more openly. He soon introduced us to his latest girlfriend, Hesu, a tall, attractive Korean woman with an oval face about half his age. One weekend, we spent the whole day with my father and Hesu, going to see a restored version of the film *Citizen Kane,* followed by dinner at a Korean restaurant, where Hesu took over. I remember how she imperiously barked orders in Korean at the cowering wait staff. I wasn't sure what Hesu did for a living, but my father joked that she enjoyed partying with members of the Rolling Stones. He would also tease her in our presence, claiming that she was a Korean War orphan whom he had rescued off the streets of Seoul. By this time, my father had moved into a studio apartment off of Madison Avenue and Sixty-third Street.

For several years I would shuttle back and forth between the apartment I lived in with my mother and brothers on the Upper West Side and my father's studio apartment on the East Side. Although they were long separated and clearly dating others, my parents still remained technically married. By the time they finally got around to the divorce in 1976, it seemed more of an afterthought. My father told the presiding civil court judge to give my mother whatever she wanted and my mother countered that she only wanted enough to live on. Noticing how amicable my parents were, the hardened judge asked, half jokingly, why they were getting a divorce.

9. A Dog in the Hunt

When I was in seventh grade, I shared with my father how intimidated I felt by my school's mercurial principal, Dr. Seamus O'Hanlon, a sandy-haired, diminutive man with a thick Irish brogue and an impish smile. "Dr. O," as we called him, was known for having a hair-trigger temper, often sending students to his office for minor infractions. Hearing my concerns, my dad's advice was simple: try to imagine Dr. O'Hanlon naked. This, he suggested, would cut him down to size and remind me that he was merely a man made of flesh and blood.

I'm sure my dad was speaking mostly metaphorically, but at the self-conscious impressionable age of thirteen, I found the prospect of picturing the tweed- and checkered-pants-wearing, elfin-like principal without any clothes on as something less than appealing, and I quickly banished that thought from my mind altogether. Still, my father's attempt to help seemed to work, and I no longer felt as intimidated by my principal, who would even become somewhat of a friend later in high school. I certainly had fewer detentions.

As the child of a successful writer growing up in the New York area of the 1960s and '70s, I was taught creative ways to deal with life's challenges. One lesson was to remain cool in the presence of famous people. From an early age, my brothers and I were accustomed to meeting and spotting celebrities of all stripes — including renowned playwrights, actors, novelists, screenwriters, musicians, and all sorts of artists — often at informal party settings where decorum required that we act like nothing was out of the ordinary. Indeed, celebrities, my dad taught us, were just normal, everyday people — albeit, successful people in their chosen profession, not unlike top doctors and lawyers. He said that we should never feel intimidated or uncomfortable in their presence — and that went equally as well for people of authority whom we encountered in everyday life. Merely flesh and blood.

I remember one Saturday night during the mid-'70s, having dinner at table number four at Elaine's with my father when, in a span of fifteen minutes, in walked, separately, Al Pacino, Robert DeNiro, and Giancarlo Giannini; sitting at the table next to ours throughout the meal was Woody Allen with a group of friends. I noticed how my father simply nodded a faint smile of recognition at his friend Allen, who returned the gesture. They both knew how to play it cool.

While many patrons occasionally glanced at Allen — and noticeably turned their heads to see the movie stars arrive — they resumed their meals with the requisite indifference. I myself may have played it a bit too cool when I ignited a red Amaretti cookie wrapper using the table's candle. I watched helplessly, my embarrassment increasing, as the wrapper dissolved into a burning ash plume and hovered, zeppelin-like, over toward Allen's head, petering out just before impact.

My father's hard-and-fast rule about always maintaining one's cool and not acting affected around celebrities was a bit slippery, we would learn, when it came to professional sports stars.

Once, while dining with my brother Drew in 1973 at Sam's, a restaurant on the Upper East Side, my father had just finished explaining that celebrities were no different than anyone else — "They're only people, Drew" — when in walked New York Knicks superstar Walt "Clyde" Frazier, dressed to the nines in a dark, brimmed Borsalino hat, black fur coat, and stylish loafers.

Frazier escorted a lady on each arm and was trailed by his driver and a coterie of friends and admirers. Indeed, Clyde's presence had a magnetic effect on nearly everyone in the popular eatery as he sauntered over to his table like visiting royalty.

When my dad turned to see what all the commotion was, his eyes lit up and he repeated in childlike rapture: "It's — Clyde! It's — Clyde! I have to go say 'Hi.'"

He then stood up and walked over, entranced as if following the Pied Piper, to Frazier's table, leaving my brother alone. Grinning from ear to ear, my father shook Frazier's hand and mumbled a few words to which Frazier good-naturedly responded. When Drew asked him what he had said to Frazier, my father was too star-struck to answer. (My father would have a similar reaction years later when he found Muhammad Ali standing next to him at an adjacent urinal in the men's bathroom at Chasen's in Hollywood. Overlooking the awkwardness of the moment, he kept chanting "Ali! Ali! You are the greatest!," all while continuing to relieve himself.)

Such was the magic and appeal that charismatic sports stars held over us that they could reduce grown men to wide-eyed little kids.

My first inkling of the emotional impact that sports stars could have occurred when I was seven and my father took us to see a Yankees game at the old Yankee Stadium in the Bronx. This was in the late summer of 1968, during the final year of Mickey Mantle's illustrious Hall of Fame career, and I'm pretty certain my father wanted my brothers and me to see "The Mick" before he retired.

I remember we had decent seats, about fifteen to twenty rows up behind home plate. At the time, I had only a faint idea who Mantle was, as I had never been to a baseball game before and had only watched a little baseball on TV. My father pointed him out to me on the field. His body thickened and hobbled by the triple-threat ravages of age, injuries, and hard living, Mantle, at thirty-six, lumbered around the bases as if in slow motion for much of the game. Still, he had an undeniable star presence, as if he knew the spotlight was squarely on him, which was probably true, since he was one of the few bright spots on a mostly dismal team; these were the fallow years, when the once-mighty Yankees franchise was reduced to being an American League doormat.

Much has been written about Mantle's tremendous upper-body strength and broad back and shoulder muscles, which seemingly stretched the outer limits of his famous pinstriped number 7 jersey. All this was plain to see as his massive frame made him stand out from the more slender athletes on the field that day. But you could also see evidence of Mantle's majesty in small, elegant gestures, like the way he casually whipped the ball around the infield as if he were playing a game of catch in his own backyard, or how he rested on one knee in the on-deck batter's box, effortlessly taking practice swings with a bat that resembled more a stickball bat than a Louisville Slugger when held in his large, meaty arms.

There was a definite charge in the air as legendary announcer Mel Allen's booming Southern drawl echoed throughout the hallowed stadium — like the voice of God calling down from the heavens — "Now batting. Number 7. Mick-ey Man-tle," that you didn't feel with the announcement of players of lesser caliber such as, say, Horace Clarke or Tom Tresh. His mobility hampered by bad knees, like many aging baseball stars Mantle was relegated to playing first base, and he seemed to be going through the motions for much of the game. Then, in the latter innings, he connected with a thunderous crack of the bat, sending a screaming line drive over the right field fence. Bleacher bums in the nearly empty cheap seats raced to collect the free memento, which they knew they could easily sell to fans for a nice profit.

As if emerging from a slumber, the crowd gave Mantle a standing ovation as he slowly trotted around the bases. He gently tipped his cap in appreciation. My dad rose too, as did my brothers and I (although I could barely see through the throng of standing people as Mantle rounded third base and headed for home), and my dad said solemnly: "Boys, remember this moment. You just saw the great Mickey Mantle hit a home run."

Yeah, it was special — even to this seven-year-old — but I also remember "The Mick" was upstaged that day by his younger, more free-spirited teammate Joe Pepitone, who slammed two homers. There would, however, be no such speech for Pepitone.

(Years later, I would take my nine-year-old son, Max, to a ball game at the old County Stadium in Milwaukee to see Baltimore Orioles star Cal Ripkin Jr. during the twilight of his Hall of Fame career. We sat in the "Diamond Box" seats, about seven rows behind home plate. When Ripkin hit a line-drive double during his first at-bat, I pointed out to Max with as much solemnity as I could muster that he had just witnessed "the Great Cal Ripkin Jr." hit a double, echoing my dad's words of nearly thirty-five years earlier. But my son, who was never much of a sports enthusiast, simply shrugged his shoulders with indifference and asked when we could leave. He showed more interest in his hand-held video game and a fat vendor hawking peanuts and popcorn in the stands, so we left shortly after the third inning.)

Another time, it was late in the fourth quarter at Madison Square Garden. The Knicks held onto a comfortable lead and the game's outcome was no longer in doubt. Even Dancin' Harry, the colorful, caped unofficial team cheerleader in platform shoes, had stopped prowling the Garden stands and casting his "whammy" hex at the opposing team's bench. In other words, it was what my dad called "garbage time."

The Rolls-Royce tandem of basketball's superstar guards, Walt "Clyde" Frazier and Earl "The Pearl" Monroe, sat comfortably on the bench, the Pearl's bright, toothy smile flashing from beneath a white towel while he clowned with teammates. Meanwhile, Clyde was a picture of typical coolness, with legs casually crossed and one arm slung absently over an empty chair — he might just as well be at the New York Ballet or spending a quiet Sunday afternoon in the park reading Chaucer.

Reserve guards Dean "The Dream" Meminger and Henry Bibby now ran the show, backed up by the likes of scrubs Mel Davis and John Gianelli (whose affable face and curly brown locks atop his six-foot-ten pencil-shaped frame reminded me of Big Bird from

Sesame Street). Even old stalwarts "Dollar" Bill Bradley and Dave "Big D" DeBusschere had taken a seat. Gangly Phil Jackson was still out there, of course — mainly for his quirky, but effective defensive skills — frenetically churning his pale, bony arms at inbound passes and projecting his gawky six-foot-eight body like a marionette on speed to disrupt the opponents' general flow of play.

A faint chant soon rose from the crowd. It began as a few random shouts and then quickly gained in strength until it reached a crescendo and the entire Garden shook to its core. My father and I joined in gustily.

"WING-GO! WING-GO!"

As if on cue, venerable Knicks coach Red Holzman gestured to a lanky player sitting on the sidelines, who quickly popped up from the bench to the obvious delight of the crowd. He tore off his white warm-up jersey with the familiar orange and blue Knicks lettering, gliding past the old coach as he made his way to the scorer's table, where he reported for duty and sat, awaiting the next stoppage in play. He was a six-foot-six phenomenon of mostly arms and legs — a sort of poor man's Dr. J — and he had quickly become a cult hero among Knicks loyalists, with a catchy name and swashbuckling, crowd-pleasing style of play. How, my dad wondered, could anyone not love a basketball player named Hawthorne Wingo? I agreed. He sounded like a character straight out of Dickens or Melville. ("Thar she blows, the great black whale, Wingo!")

Wingo would not disappoint. Shortly after entering the game, he made one of his familiar mad-dash runs to the basket. Gripping the basketball in his oversized hand like a grapefruit, he swooped in like a hawk, wheeling and coiling his angular body, leaving defenders in his wake as his outstretched arm circled around the rim of the basket, executing a circus-like dunk. We joined the crowd in showing our appreciation, resuming the chant:

"WING-GO! WING-GO!"

Hawthorne Wingo was just one in a long line of sports figures who occupied my childhood years. Cheering wildly for the unlikeliest of sports personalities was one of the most enjoyable ways of passing the time, especially in the sports-mad town of New York. It didn't matter the caliber of the player, or even the sport, although we much preferred when our favorite athlete and team were successful.

My dad said that watching sports meant a lot more when you had "a dog in the hunt," meaning an athlete or team in contention for the championships. But often it was simply fun to root for someone who had a superior athletic ability, or maybe a quirky style of play that caught your eye. Sometimes it was as simple as a player's unusual name, like Mr. Wingo's. Another favorite name of my dad's at the time was a reserve baseball outfielder from Puerto Rico named Bombo Rivera, who didn't even play for a New York team; he just loved hearing the sound of his name: "Now batting, Bombo Rivera."

My father and I could just as easily be amused by the activities that occurred off the playing field. For instance, he saved some of his choicest comments for whenever Knicks forward Phil Jackson caused a stoppage in play — which seemed to happen often — while searching on his hands and knees for an errant contact lens on the court at the Garden. I think my dad could relate because he wore hard contact lenses and occasionally dropped them at the most inopportune times. At boxing matches he paid equal attention to the side work in between rounds, as corner men worked feverishly to stanch cuts or offer tactical advice to their fighter.

Considering all the sporting events my father took me and my brothers to (as well as numerous outings to plays, restaurants, amusement parks, and individual and family trips to Hollywood and Disneyworld), it's a wonder he was so productive in his writing career during our childhood — churning out dozens of short stories, two successful plays, several novels, and movie and TV scripts. But sports was such a vital part of the social fabric of the greater New York area that it was unavoidable that one would be caught up in the excitement, and we loved rooting for our favorite teams and stars as much as hearing about our father's childhood sports heroes.

We were fortunate to live in the New York area during the late 1960s and '70s because there was never a shortage of competitive teams and athletes from various professional sports to root for, and one could always count on a colorful cast of emerging and old reliable stars. There was, indeed, always "a dog in the hunt." And as championships go, from 1969 through '73, New York was at the epicenter of the U.S. sports world and could boast a championship team in just about all major professional sports.

While the Knicks were tearing up the league on the way to their first of two NBA titles (1970 and 1973), the upstart Jets of the American Football League — under the brash and brilliant "Broadway Joe" Namath — pulled off one the greatest upsets in sports history when they beat the heavily favored Baltimore Colts in Super Bowl III in 1969.

Meanwhile, in Flushing Meadows, Queens, in the backdrop of the 1964 World's Fair grounds, the overachieving young New York

Mets were providing their own fireworks over at Shea Stadium, winning the baseball World Series in 1969 against the heavily favored Baltimore Orioles. They would return to the World Series in 1973, but lose in seven games to the Oakland Athletics. My father managed to score tickets for me and my brothers to see the "Amazing Mets" win Game 3 of the '69 World Series at Shea Stadium — on a school day, no less! Even the lowly New York Rangers were knocking on the door of the National Hockey League's grandest prize, the Stanley Cup, although, sadly, they would fall short in 1972 to the powerhouse Boston Bruins.

About this time, I began avidly flipping and trading sports cards with my Great Neck neighbors and schoolmates. I remember trading cards with a boy named Irwin and his younger brother, who lived in a palatial home a block away. I developed an impressive collection of baseball cards of my own, starting with the 1967 season. Irwin and his brother had a wide range of football, hockey, and oversized basketball cards that I had not seen before. I was fortunate to have many extra New York Mets cards from the '69 World Series team, which were all the rage, especially the much-coveted Tom Seaver card. I would eagerly exchange my baseball cards for the more unfamiliar cards and pretty soon I would acquire a full set of Knicks cards, including just about all the NBA stars. Unfortunately, Irwin had written his name across many of his sports cards, so my Lew Alcindor rookie card (before he converted to Islam and changed his name to Kareem Abdul-Jabbar) had a great big "Irwin" written across the middle, rendering the card worthless. But I didn't mind. I also enjoyed all the many NFL and NHL cards I collected, with names of athletes I had never heard of before, such as Gump Worsley of the Montreal

Canadiens. Gump was one of the old-school veteran hockey goalies who eschewed wearing a facemask, thinking it unmanly, and he had a chewed-up, battered mug to thank for it.

I loved listening to my father tell us the stories of his childhood sports heroes. My father grew up in the Bronx, "in the shadow of Yankee Stadium," as he liked to put it. Despite the machine-like efficiency and success of the Yankees during his childhood, he said he was more a fan of the scrappy, ragtag Brooklyn Dodgers and would often take the subway to Ebbets Field at the opposite end of the city just to catch a glimpse of his childhood heroes Pee Wee Reese, Dixie Walker, Carl Furillo, and especially Jackie Robinson. He also had the luxury of watching his next favorite team, the New York Giants, at the old Polo Grounds just fifteen minutes away across the Harlem River, in Upper Manhattan. Our perennially tanned grandfather, Poppy, was the Yankees fan. Poppy had been watching Yankees games since the days of Babe Ruth and Lou Gehrig, mostly sunning himself in the cheap bleacher seats.

My interest in sports was more global than my father's. I enjoyed professional hockey and the emergence of the New York Islanders. I also followed the 1972 World Cup of soccer and, like much of New York, fell in love with the great Brazilian star, Pelé, who singlehandedly placed that sport on the U.S. map, especially after he joined the New York Cosmos. It inspired me and a legion of other New York teens to take up soccer and play throughout our high school years.

My father would shrug his shoulders and tell me he only had room for certain sports in his busy schedule: baseball, basketball, boxing, and football — plus the occasional "Breakfast at Wimbledon" tennis championship. Another sport he had no time for was golf, which, he joked, you couldn't pay him enough to watch. He would put that theory to the test, declining a lucrative offer to ghostwrite a professional golfer's memoir.

Still, I would test my father's patience for watching unusual sports on a number of occasions. At age twelve, I developed a fondness for professional wrestling, quickly amassing as many wrestling magazines as possible. I remember scouring the New York TV stations late at night and on weekends, searching for any wrestling programs. I especially enjoyed shows that featured less familiar, exotic, regional wrestlers from across the United States — such as in Florida and Texas, where wrestling took on a rebellious, wildcat-like flavor (not unlike early NASCAR, I suspect).

I remember watching hours of Lucha Libre — Mexican-style acrobatic wrestling with more of a carnival atmosphere — on Spanish-language California TV stations whenever our father would take us out to Hollywood on business trips. Many of the wrestlers wore masks and would enter the ring dressed in colorful, feathered outfits — not unlike what I imagined Aztec warriors looked like — amid the pomp and ceremony of blasted recorded fiesta music, as if they were entering a bullfighting ring or circus tent.

I was at that magic stage in a boy's life when wrestling seemed as real as rain. I bought into the whole good guy/bad guy premise and would fret whenever a referee was distracted while a favorite wrestler was being pummeled. I believed the hyperbolic pronouncements from announcers when they said that certain dangerous wrestling moves were "banned in twelve states." Like a lot of testosterone-driven teen boys, I would even mimic my favorite wrestler's moves, such as Chief Jay Strongbow's famous "Sleeper" chokehold, once applying it to my best friend Bruce Altman's younger brother Steven, whose face turned purple as he nearly passed out.

Among my favorite wrestlers at the time were the longtime champ Bruno Sammartino (who could lift and body slam just about every wrestler atop his massive, broad shoulders, including André the Giant!), Pedro Morales, Mil Máscaras (the masked Mexican *luchador*), and the aforementioned Chief Jay Strongbow (whose real name was Joe Scarpa, from Philadelphia), who wore a traditional headdress and would employ a "Tomahawk Chop" with his open hand across his opponents' necks. On the brink of defeat, the Chief would go into an exaggerated (nowadays politically incorrect) war dance, which was more akin to a drunken sailor trying to maintain balance, before knocking off his opponent with his patented "Sleeper" hold.

Some of my favorite wrestling villains included the mysterious wrestler/manager Mr. Fuji (who dressed in a bowler and dark suit like "Odd Job" in *Goldfinger*) and his charge — and sometimes wrestling partner — Professor Toru Tanaka (I never knew what he was a professor of), who blew salt in unsuspecting opponents' eyes, perpetuating the stereotype that Japanese were sneaky and not to be trusted. Then there was the bald, enigmatic, Neanderthal-like George "The Animal" Steele who, for some reason, enjoyed chewing the stuffing from the ring turnbuckles. Incongruously, Steele led a double life as a mild-mannered high school science teacher and football coach in suburban Michigan.

Another favorite villain was Killer Kowalski, who had gained notoriety for once severing an opponent's ear with his "razor-sharp" elbow while mistiming a jump from the top of the turnbuckle. The tanned, platinum-haired "Classy" Freddie Blassie looked more like a retiree in Miami Beach than a wrestler. He had a penchant for loud sports jackets, tropical shirts, checkered pants, and white loafers, which reminded me of a beefed-up, baritone-voiced version of my grandfather Papa in Fort Lauderdale. Blassie would deride opponents and critics alike with his "pencil-necked geek" catchphrase.

Because of my exposure to the fat men and women at Coney Island amusement park freak shows during my youth, I naturally gravitated toward wrestling's big men, including the four-hundred-plus-pound Gorilla Monsoon, and the even more gargantuan six-hundred-pound Haystacks Calhoun, a hillbilly-like wrestler who wore a rope with a horseshoe around his neck and the biggest pair of blue overalls I had ever seen in my life.

The parade of colorful wrestlers — both good guys and heels — was seemingly endless, crossing all ethnic and cultural stereotypes. Amidst the backdrop of the Cold War and the Mideast oil embargo, new villains would emerge like "The Sheik," playing on people's jingoistic fears. The Sheik routinely cut opponent's faces with hidden pencils and threw fireballs into their faces. Naturally, a Communist Russian villain would soon appear as well, Nikolai Volkoff (of Croatian origin), who would vie for wrestling supremacy over our American Champion, Bruno Sammartino, who was actually born in the small town of Pizzoferrato in the Abruzzo region of Italy.

If hockey, soccer, and golf barely registered a blip on my father's sports radar, then professional wrestling was completely off the screen. Still, for two consecutive months in early 1973, he bravely took me to back-to-back wrestling shows at the Garden, where we sat near ringside. I'm sure the only enjoyment he derived from the matches — besides indulging his youngest son — was the freak show-like nature of the performers themselves and the colorful audience they attracted; I remember him commenting on how all of New York's doormen, elevator operators, and maintenance workers seemed to be in attendance at the near-capacity shows.

As quickly as my love of wrestling developed, I lost interest. I think this was due in part to my dad taking me to a night of boxing at the old Felt Forum in the spring of 1974. Perhaps he thought that viewing the "sweet science" up close would help exorcise the wrestling demons from my system. Months earlier, he had taken my older brother Josh to see Ali vs. Frazier II at the Garden, so I jumped at the opportunity to see live boxing. He had told me stories of when his father and uncle had taken him as a child to watch boxing matches in smoky, dimly lit social halls in the Bronx. He would incorporate some of those childhood memories into a fictional short story, "The Night Boxing Ended," that would appear in *GQ* magazine. From the opening bell, I was hooked. Unlike the staged and carnival feel of "professional" wrestling, I sensed there was nothing inauthentic about boxing.

Headlining the card that night was a heavyweight bout between Randy Neumann and Chuck "The Bayonne Bleeder" Wepner (Sylvester Stallone's inspiration for future *Rocky* movies), who would live up to his colorful moniker that night. By the seventh round both fighters were bloodied beyond recognition and the fight was mercifully called in Wepner's favor.

We also saw future middleweight champion Vito Antuofermo take apart a young southpaw, John L. Sullivan, named after the late-nineteenth-century bare-knuckled champion. My dad told me that fighters who took on the names of former champions rarely fared as well as their namesakes. As an example, he said, the great Sugar Ray Robinson once destroyed another fighter who had the audacity to adopt the nickname "Sugar." When Robinson was asked after the fight why he delivered such an uncharacteristic beating, he famously quipped: "Ain't but one Sugar." (Years later, Sugar Ray Leonard would prove to be the rare exception.)

Following my boxing initiation, I was fortunate enough to view with my dad arguably some of the finest heavyweight championship boxing matches of the late twentieth century: "The Rumble in the Jungle" in Zaire between Muhammad Ali and George Foreman (broadcast via closed circuit at Radio City Music Hall); "The Thrilla in Manila" epic final battle in the Ali vs. Frazier trilogy (at the Felt Forum); and Ali vs. Ken Norton III (again at the Felt Forum). Besides those seminal boxing matches, I would cajole my father into taking me to see the embarrassing Evil Knievel Snake Canyon rocket jump fiasco in 1974, which was pure spectacle devoid of all sport.

Over time, my father and I stopped attending live sporting events, preferring the ease and comfort of watching sports on TV. Following my parents' amicable divorce in 1976, I moved in with my father, who had been living alone on East Sixty-third Street in Manhattan. During this transitional time for both of us, we spent many nights eating take-out pizza in front of the Sony Trinitron TV in the living room, watching the aging Knicks, who were now in steady decline. But there would also be hope with the re-emergence of the Yankees, quickly being rebuilt by owner George Steinbrenner, who went on a buying spree, acquiring some of baseball's biggest superstars. The acquisition of the great home run slugger Reggie Jackson would prove to be the final piece of the puzzle, securing consecutive World Series titles for the Yankees after more than a decade of futility — a dominance that continues to this day. Once more there would be "a dog in the hunt."

Such was the impact of sports on my life that I can easily cite the exact moment a part of my childhood ended: October 7, 1977 — my seventeenth birthday, and more importantly, the date the Knicks shipped my childhood hero Walt "Clyde" Frazier off to the lowly Cleveland Cavaliers, which, to me, was basketball's version of Siberia. I truly believe that the Knicks have been a cursed team ever since that ignoble move (akin to the Boston Red Sox trading Bade Ruth to the Yankees) and have yet to recover. (For those who don't believe me, just say the name John Starks, or better yet, Isiah Thomas!)

One small consolation I would take from Frazier's trade was seeing his triumphant return to the Garden one month later. Dressed in an unfamiliar red and yellow Cavalier road uniform, Clyde single-handedly dismantled the rudderless Knicks roster, receiving standing ovations from the crowd before and after the game. Decades later, I'm happy to still see Clyde's debonair smile on TV commercials — and on the bottle of the "Just for Men" line of hair color products, a lasting reminder of lost innocence as well as my own graying, receding hairline. My father, on the other hand, is not so lucky. He gets to hear Clyde provide his own unique brand of color commentary as an announcer for the still-mediocre Knicks, providing awkward rhyming phrases and creative word usages called "Clyde-isms" that stretch the boundaries of the English language.

I still think my father — like many old-time Knicks fans — would react in childlike awe if he were to run into Clyde today. I know

I would. Recently, my father shared another Clyde story with me from the past. He had once spotted him in the mid-'70s at Elaine's. Naturally, my father followed him to the bar where he overheard Clyde ask the bartender in a surprisingly high-pitched voice, "Where the action at?" to which the incredulous bartender responded: "You *are* the action!"

10. It All Goes in the Soup

A Twentieth Century Food Odyssey

On the Fourth of July in 1976, with much of Manhattan caught up in the fervor of the nation's Bicentennial celebrations, my father was more interested in tandoori chicken than tall ships and fireworks.

Ever the foodie, he had been taking us to Gaylord's, a popular London restaurant specializing in North Indian cuisine, ever since it had opened a branch in Midtown Manhattan around 1972. The heavily spiced masalas and clay pot oven-cooked marinated meats and buttered breads were like a revelation — reminiscent, he said, of the unbridled joy he felt when, as a teen, he took his first bite of a cheeseburger following a steady diet of bland kosher food served by my grandmother Nanny to my grandfather Poppy, who complained of a weak stomach. (Nanny was wise to Poppy, who would nibble at his food, then slip around the corner to a diner for liver and onions and come home only to complain about his belly "problem." "I knew it," she'd say. "You just had that lousy liver and onions!") I suspect that ever since that first cheeseburger, my father has been somewhat adventurous when it came to food.

One of my father's favorite expressions I overheard while growing up was, "It all goes in the soup," a catch-all phrase that I took to mean: no matter what curveballs life throws at you, there's usually something positive you can take away from the experience — which basically summed up his generally optimistic outlook on life. But this phrase could just as easily apply to his endless passion for food, for he had a knack for picking up on the latest food trends and hot new restaurants, often heaping praise on a particular dish he had recently tried and loved. Fortunately for us, he enjoyed sharing his new culinary finds with our family whenever possible.

I'm not saying my father was overly obsessive about food. He was no precursor to one of those food bloggers who can tell you where to find the finest quality Kobe beef and foie gras sliders. We were just brought up with the understanding that enjoying good food and eating out at restaurants was one of life's many pleasures, especially if you were fortunate enough to live in the New York City area — as exciting as, say, catching Walt "Clyde" Frazier in a Knicks game at the Garden, watching Zero Mostel perform in a new play on Broadway, or riding the Cyclone roller coaster at Coney Island amusement park in Brooklyn.

Food in all its varieties was part of the cultural landscape. As usual, my father's early hunch about Gaylord's proved correct, and we added the new Indian restaurant to our ever-expanding list of favorite dining spots. On subsequent visits, the friendly turbaned maître d' would greet me with all the fanfare typically reserved for a raja. "Hello, Mr. Kips," he would say cheerfully with an exaggerated sweep of the arm as he led us to our table; I suspect he remembered my name because of its similarity to Rudyard Kipling.

New York City can be an overwhelming and intimidating place, but even more so when you're young. To me as a child, it resembled the fabled Emerald City in the movie *The Wizard of Oz* as we drove in from Glen Cove, and then later from Great Neck, Long Island, before finally moving to the Upper West Side of Manhattan in the fall of 1972. My earliest memories of Manhattan are from the relative safety of the backseat of the family's white Buick sedan, driving along the Long Island Expressway, staring out at the endless skyline and bridges connecting the city to the outer boroughs. The view made me think of the medieval castles, drawbridges, and moats that I played with in my brother Drew's room. I marveled at the police officers who towered above our car astride majestic massive horses like blue Knights of the Round Table as they worked crowd control along Broadway and Times Square.

Notwithstanding my initial fairy tale impressions of the city, Manhattan in the mid-'60s through the early '70s was clearly not the Disney World-like theme park that it has become today. Nightmarish scenes also remain fixed in my mind. I remember dope dealers, strung-out junkies, and inebriated bums sprawled out on sidewalks or staggering aimlessly like zombies along the Bowery. (Was this the fate that awaited those loveable losers depicted in the Bowery Boys films of the 1940s and '50s that we watched religiously on weekend television?)

I also remember heavily rouged, bewigged prostitutes (both male and female) in bright colored "hot pants" and high heels and platform shoes flagging down motorists and offering "dates" to passersby, all while casting a wary eye for the inevitable police cruiser in a nighttime game of cat-and-mouse along the Hell's Kitchen section of the West

Side. Then there were the colorful pimps, with their unique brand of sartorial finery, hovering about like some subspecies of mutant urban superheroes alongside flashy Cadillac Eldorados and Lincoln Continentals, otherwise known as "pimpmobiles."

Amidst this otherwise scary and unpredictable environment — combined with the backdrop of my parents' failing marriage — food would serve as a sort of equalizer for me, providing more than mere nourishment, but also comfort and stability. It was hard to imagine Manhattan without also conjuring the homey, familiar smells that literally assaulted your olfactory senses once you crossed over the Triborough Bridge into the city.

My brothers and I were drawn like magnets to the pleasant aromas of the street foods sold by vendors under bright yellow umbrellas on most city corners: warm oversized salted pretzels on rings; hot roasted peanuts; foot-long hot dogs plucked from vats of opaque, greasy water and then lathered in mustard and sauerkraut; and sweet, fragrant chestnuts roasting over an open fire and then dispensed in little brown paper wrappers (this was long before the advent of the food truck phenomenon, with their dizzying array of fusion foods like kimchi tacos and duck fat french fries in truffle oil).

By mimicking my brothers, I learned early on how to handle a piping hot slice of pizza at curbside pizza parlors, folding the crust into a wedge held firmly between thumb and forefinger. The trick was to start eating from the narrowest point and work your way slowly back toward the middle, allowing your free hand to catch the slice if it started to droop, which it rarely did. With mozzarella flowing like lava and a trickle of oil dripping onto thin wax paper, the triangular-shaped slice of heaven would typically burn the roof of my mouth, but the burn was always worth it. As every New Yorker will proudly tell you, there's something about the local water that makes the pizza dough taste so special and unique. Having lived all across the country, I've yet to encounter a pizza that consistently surpasses the humble New York slice.

(Once, while eating at a Dallas pizzeria with my brother Josh, a large bearded man in a stained apron came over and asked in a Texas drawl what we thought of his "New Yawk pizza." I suspect he had overheard us earlier discuss how mediocre the pizza was, and he was feeling a bit defensive. The excessively doughy slices barely had a crust, the cheese had coagulated into little white amoeba-like splotches, and the sauce tasted flavorless. Not wishing to offend him, though, I responded: "Well, it's not New York pizza. But it's not Los Angeles, either — It's Dallas pizza." The man's brow furrowed, and he soon returned with several cups of ranch salad dressing in which to dip the half-eaten slices of pizza, suggesting that this would liven up the flavor. "That's disgusting!" uttered my brother with disdain, pushing aside the cups of salad dressing. The owner's face darkened, and I was afraid a fight might ensue. Only when Josh told him that he was a boxer in training, and to let us eat in peace, did the man finally retreat, although he would continue to glare at us from behind the counter.)

It's no secret that New York City is a food lover's paradise. One could spend a lifetime here and merely scratch the surface of the changing culinary landscape. New restaurants come and go like Off-Broadway plays, to be replaced by the latest production. On the heels of the Indian food explosion of the early '70s, with Indian and Pakistani restaurants soon becoming as ubiquitous as pizzerias and delis, came the new wave of Szechuan and Hunan cuisine, led by pioneering restaurants like Uncle Tai's Hunan Yuan, which introduced bold, smoky flavors with a heavy emphasis on whole dried chili pods and fresh green chilies, peppercorns, and garlic.

These were clearly not your grandparents' Chinese restaurants; they turned up the volume on more traditional Americanized Cantonese food. New Yorkers were abandoning old standards like General Tso's chicken and moo goo gai pan for more exotic dishes like fiery, crispy orange beef and stir-fried green beans in hot chili sauce. One memorable new dish unlike anything we had ever experienced before was Uncle Tai's diced squab and peanuts served in lettuce wraps (a watered down version is now a mainstay at most P.F. Chang's). Naturally, my father knew where to go for the best sweat-producing Szechuan and Hunan restaurants.

I couldn't get over the dizzying array of ethnic restaurants in such proximity to one another: Indian, Chinese, Pakistani, Japanese, Lebanese, Thai, Italian, French, Spanish, Belgian, Austrian, Swiss, Danish, Greek, Armenian, Israeli, Egyptian, Turkish, and more, in an ever-changing combination of ethnicities from street to street. It felt like we were living among a shifting mini-United Nations, co-existing in relative peace despite any tensions a world away. (In fact, the restaurants were even safer than the UN, as I was to learn while on a seventh grade field trip when a classmate thoughtlessly set off a smoke bomb in the men's bathroom of the UN, causing chaos and an immediate evacuation of the entire building.) If there's a distinct cuisine somewhere in the farthest, most remote region of the world, there's a good chance that it will eventually show up on a menu or food emporium in New York City.

When you look at a map of Manhattan, it even looks somewhat like a porterhouse steak, with Central Park running down the middle like an oversized T-bone. Brooklyn and Queens interlace like a more marbled, flavorful ribeye steak just across the narrow East River.

Manhattan became more familiar, and palatable, when broken down into distinct neighborhoods: the Broadway theater area in the tenderloin of the city, with its famous pre-theater restaurants like Frankie & Johnnie's, the popular steakhouse, and Sardi's, renowned for its show-business celebrity caricatures festooned across its walls; the grittier, but immensely flavorful, Chinatown, Little Italy, and hippie-inspired East and West Village restaurants in Lower Manhattan; the funkier Hispanic restaurants of the Upper West Side; and the more tony, upscale continental and French establishments near Midtown and on the Upper East Side.

Like most big cities, there are entire blocks in Manhattan devoted to a single ethnic cuisine. Everyone knows about Little Italy and Chinatown, but natives also enjoy areas like Koreaway on Thirty-second Street between Fifth Avenue and Broadway (in the heart of Koreatown) for some of the best Korean bulgogi barbecue around, typically prepared, self-serve style, on tableside built-in grills. My father's Korean girlfriend in the mid-'70s, Hesu, used to take us to one particular restaurant in Koreatown called Arirang, where we discovered the joy of garlicky, sweet-and-sour mandu meatball dumplings.

My brother Drew spent much of the '80s living in a tenement-era walk-up flat on East Sixth Street, otherwise known as "Curry Row" for its multitude of Indian and Pakistani restaurants. We used to joke that the twenty-plus restaurants on his block were all serviced by one long conveyor belt, although, in truth, each restaurant had its own distinct regional influence. His block often felt more like Mumbai than Manhattan, with colorfully dressed, turbaned barkers inviting you into each restaurant and the sound of sitars, tambours, and flutes spilling out onto the street.

When the mood hit us for some authentic German food, we'd visit the Upper East Side Yorkville section of Manhattan. A favorite spot was the Heidelberg Restaurant with its distinct alpine brown-and-white frontage off of East Eighty-sixth Street. In the '30s, this area was known as "the German Broadway" and was infamous for its German-American Bund rallies where goose-stepping celebrants marched proudly in Nazi insignia shouting "Sieg heil!" and giving Hitler salutes — something my dad would note, a bit too loudly, while digging into heaping plates of Wiener schnitzel, red cabbage, and spaetzle served by wait staff dressed in Bavarian lederhosen.

My father has always had a gift for embellishment, making things sound more magical and exciting than perhaps they actually were — which is one of the reasons why he has had such a long and successful writing career. How could we fault him, then, when he would apply this trait to food? Like spices, his descriptions only served to enhance the flavors of most meals and food experiences, making the ordinary extraordinary, and memorable. He was also fully aware of how words could be misused to exaggerate the impact on food. For instance, whenever he saw a restaurant promoting itself as "world famous" — say, "world-famous waffles" — he would question, jokingly, whether the waffles really were renowned in Africa or Asia.

One of our favorite food-related stories my father used to share with us involved his friend and fraternity brother, Skippy, at the

University of Missouri. My father said Skippy would ask if he could eat the fat and gristle left over on people's plates. Skippy would insist, over any objections, that the fat tasted much better than the meat. At restaurants, Skippy would even specifically order a plate of fat, instructing the waiter to remove any trace of meat. We couldn't believe that someone would purposely bypass the choicest parts of a steak in order to zero in on the fat, but that's apparently what sustained Skippy throughout college.

Another story I believed was that my father's scrambled eggs — adding a splash of milk with a dash of salt and pepper and then whisking thoroughly in a bowl — had gained him fame and recognition while serving as a First Lieutenant in the U.S. Air Force.

("On behalf of the entire United States Air Force, please accept this special commendation, First Lieutenant Friedman, for your outstanding service to our nation in preparing those delicious New Yuk-style scrambled eggs.")

Whether his technique actually was renowned in the Air Force (or even made the eggs taste any better) is negligible — and beside the point; it's something that I have not forgotten, and I have passed on his scrambled egg preparation to my son.

Dishes that I would never actually get to taste, and restaurants that I would never visit, still remain in my mind thanks to my father's vivid descriptions — that's how real they seemed to me.

For instance, he used to tell me of a special soup — a variation of hot borscht served with Russian dumplings and other secret ingredients — available only for lunch on Wednesdays at the now defunct Russian Tea Room on West Fifty-seventh Street. The soup was so revered, he said, that well-heeled customers and power brokers from around the world were known to fly in on private jets just to get their weekly fix and then depart later that day.

He also raved about a Midtown Chinese restaurant called Pearl's, where the imperious proprietress, Madam Pearl, would size up customers at the door and inform them — if they were fortunate enough to get a table that night — what they would be served rather than allowing them to foolishly order for themselves. She never failed to present something unique and marvelous. My father still speaks reverently of Pearl's lemon chicken.

I could only dream about such now-defunct Midtown temples to French gastronomy that were beloved by my father — Le Cirque, La Caravelle, and Lutece (though Drew and I did take our mother and our wives to Lutece for a memorable meal in 2004, months before its closing).

I recall my father once being particularly animated after having dinner at his friend Mario Puzo's house in Hicksville, Long Island. He and my father shared a passion for food. (While on a family vacation in Puerto Rico, we sought out a particular restaurant in Old San Juan that was renowned for its seafood paella based solely on Puzo's recommendation.) Puzo's wife had prepared a Sicilian-style braciole — a pork roulade mixed with Italian spices, cheese, prosciutto, and bread crumbs, and then slowly baked in its own juices with olive oil. Meanwhile, Puzo, dressed in a wifebeater undershirt — in a scene reminiscent of Peter "Fat Pete" Clemenza in *The Godfather* — stirred a large pot of spaghetti until it was cooked al dente while preparing a red sauce. My father said the meal was one of the most delicious he had ever tasted.

My father did, however, take me a few times to the Dallas Cowboy restaurant, which opened in New York about a year after the Dallas

Cowboys' first Super Bowl victory in 1971. The restaurant, which specialized in authentic Texas-style chili (tomato-free with dried chili peppers, a smoky flavor, and ground sirloin), was established by the owner of the Dallas Cowboys. He was particularly taken with the fact that the chili was said to be flown in daily from Texas.

Food, for me, has always been synonymous with family. My earliest food memories coincide with trips to my grandparents' apartment in the Bronx, typically to observe Passover or the High Holidays, often in the company of our Aunt Dollie, Uncle Irving, and cousins Chuck and Scott, who lived in Fair Lawn, New Jersey. Like most Jewish families, food would play a central role in these gatherings.

Moments after stepping from the elevator, even before we reached their apartment, we could smell the burning schmaltz — chicken fat — that Nanny, my grandmother, was using to fry up her potato pancakes with chopped onions. As overpowering as that smell was, a secondary smell hit us as we entered their apartment: that of chopped chicken livers also sautéing in schmaltz. My brothers and I would each grab a potato pancake off a short stack separated by layers of greasy paper towels resting on a plate by the stove. Potato pancakes and chopped chicken livers were about as exotic as Nanny was allowed to cook due to Poppy's supposed weak stomach.

The main course usually featured a slab of boiled brisket or a boiled, pale chicken with matzoh ball soup and kreplach (meat-filled dumplings) accompanied by a plate of kasha varnishkes (buckwheat groats with farfel noodles and mushrooms). Other than the potato pancakes, my favorite part of the meal was usually dessert. My grandmother purchased jellied mini fruit slices, kosher macaroons, and an assortment of cookies from a local Italian bakery.

To this day, my single favorite dessert still remains the green, yellow, and red rainbow cookies Nanny first introduced to me when I was around 3 or 4 years old. Rainbow cookies are my madeleine sponge cakes, made famous by Proust in *Remembrance of Things Past*. They never fail to transport me instantly to a distant past in my grandparents' musty apartment in the Bronx or the living room of my aunt and uncle's tri-level home in New Jersey. To me, rainbow cookies are the perfect confection. Brilliantly combining an array of bright colors with wonderful tastes, they resemble little Italian flags covered in chocolate, with each almond-flavored spongy layer separated by apricot and raspberry jam. Aunt Dollie would carry on the family tradition of delivering a box of rainbow cookies long after my grandmother's passing in 1972, and no trip to New York is complete for me without a slice of pizza and some rainbow cookies.

It was only when we ate out, though, that food became truly exciting. It was also a means for me to learn more about our family's history and, by extension, the history of Manhattan. My father used to take us to Horn & Hardart, one of New York's few remaining automat cafeteria-style restaurants. At one time there were dozens of automats throughout Manhattan and the East Coast, offering the convenience of countless choices of prepared hot and cold foods, which patrons would pay for by placing coins in slots, turning chrome-plated knobs, and watching as little glass window slots would (miraculously, to me) slowly open. My father would relate how during the Depression years of the '30s, when money was scarce, people would come to the Automat and order a cup of hot water and then ask for ketchup and saltine crackers in order to make homemade tomato soup.

Another restaurant we occasionally visited was Ratner's, a Jewish kosher dairy restaurant on Second Avenue in the East Village, next door to the old Fillmore East concert hall (the original Ratner's was on Delancey Street in the heart of the predominantly Jewish Lower East Side). Here we would get our fill of such Jewish soul food as blintzes, potato pancakes, mushroom and barley soup, pirogen, beet borsht, onion rolls, gefilte fish — all downed with an old-fashioned bottle of seltzer water with a screw-on top, along with a plate of pickled sour green tomatoes and hot red peppers. These were the comfort foods familiar to my grandparents and countless other Jewish immigrant families from Eastern Europe that filled the Lower East Side tenements and streets at the turn of the twentieth century.

My grandfather's real name was Irving, but I grew up believing that he was called Poppy because of his love of everything poppy seed related — from Hungarian bittersweet poppy seed tortes and rolls to poppy seed bagels and poppy seed/prune hamentashen (triangular fruit-filled little cookies, usually made on the Jewish holiday of Purim). To this day, I have a soft spot for anything prepared with poppy seeds because it makes me feel a special connection with my beloved grandfather. My father used to call Poppy a famous "bread man" as well because of his hearty appetite for bread. This led me to imagine that there were scores of people in the Bronx who would see him and say things like, "There goes a true bread man." My father also called me a "soup man," making me feel special and that I, too, had a legion of admirers for my reputation as a lover of soups.

If I was a "soup man," then I blame Nanny, who first introduced me to a cup of hot and sour soup when I was about six at Ruby Foo's, an old-time Chinese restaurant on Broadway in Times Square.

Nanny told me that when my father was a child he also enjoyed the hot and sour soup at Ruby Foo's. Expecting the more bland egg drop soup, I started coughing after the first taste of the thick peppery, sour soup, but I was instantly hooked. (Years later, I would introduce hot and sour soup to my son, Max, and it was with a swelling of pride that I read a seventh grade essay in which he wrote: "I consider myself a gourmand of sorts, and I enjoy a nice bowl of hot and sour soup now and then.")

Whenever we visited my father's Midtown office at Magazine Management Company, where he worked as an editor of men's adventure magazines, we would stop afterwards for lunch or dinner. One of his favorite restaurants in the area was Xochitl's (pronounced "so-sheels," which translates as "flower" in Aztec language), a sparsely decorated hole-in-the-wall specializing in authentic Mexico City tacos and other street foods. My mother always ordered for dessert a wedge of guava jelly with a Mexican cream cheese, something I shied away from — preferring flan or Mexican fried ice cream — but now would love to try.

Another restaurant we visited was Il Cortile on Mulberry Street in the heart of Little Italy, which featured a dessert that I did try — and hated at the time, although I now treasure it — called torta di ricotta (ricotta cheesecake). My father would savor each bite of the complex grainy cheesecake — which included preserved fruit rinds and nuts, with hints of rum, almond flavoring, and orange/lemon zest, topped by a light dusting of powdery sugar — all the while sipping from a small cup of strong espresso, rubbing a lemon peel against the rim to counteract the bitterness of the over-roasted coffee. Satisfied, he would then top off his meal with a cigar.

On Thanksgiving in 1967, when I was seven, my father took the entire family to The Four Seasons restaurant to celebrate the success of his Off-Broadway hit play *Scuba Duba*. The play had opened a month earlier to rave reviews from *The New York Times* and other newspapers. This was a little more than a year after he left his day job of over thirteen years at Magazine Management Company.

Quitting his job to write a play must have been a huge gamble, fraught with many challenges and no guarantee of success — especially with a wife and three pre-teenage sons and a mortgage. Close friends of his had written plays that closed in one night after a devastating review by Clive Barnes in *The New York Times*. I can only imagine the stress he was under as he sweated out the entire production, from finding funding to securing the right venue (New York's New Theatre) to selecting just the right cast. (He chose Jerry Orbach for the play's lead and Judd Hirsch and Cleavon Little, among others, for supporting roles. I later learned that a then-unknown pre-*The Graduate* Dustin Hoffman had literally begged him to be the lead, but my father stuck by the Bronx-born Orbach.) Rewrites to the script were made right up to opening night, and perhaps afterwards.

To make matters worse, the play's original director quit and had to be replaced within months of opening night. With more than a bit of irony, the play was billed as a "tense comedy." One can forgive my father then for being in a particularly effusive and celebratory mood during our 1967 Thanksgiving meal at The Four Seasons. When it was time for dessert, the waiter wheeled out an entire chocolate cake covered in thick sheets of dark chocolate. When the waiter saw my eyes light up, he offered me the entire cake and my father (winking) said sure, put it on the bill. (I was only a little bit disappointed when I couldn't find the cake in the refrigerator.)

My father used to tell us the story of how when Walter Matthau, who had been a poor, struggling actor in New York during his early career, finally scored a success on Broadway, the first thing he did was buy an entire sturgeon at Zabar's. Apparently, this was Matthau's way of exorcising his demons from those lean years when buying mere lox was an extravagance. My father, no doubt, was thinking of Walter Matthau and Zabar's that Thanksgiving night in 1967.

As usual, though, his eyes would pop when he was presented with the bill. This was a recurrent gag he performed throughout our childhood. When handed the bill, he would nonchalantly take a look, do a double take, and then gasp. After clearing his throat and wiping his brow, he would then say, reassuringly, that everything was okay. (He also used to joke that the first French words my brothers and I learned when we took a family vacation to France in the summer of 1965 were: "Give the bill to him.")

Four decades later, I would receive a postcard from my father while he was vacationing in Paris. The card showed the rooftops of Paris and came with a brief message: "You'd love the soups here."

Nothing more needed to be said. All those years later, I was still a famous "soup man" in his eyes.

It is now up to me to travel to France to see for myself if I will, indeed, love the soups there.

11. What's in a Name?

Had I been born a girl my mother would have named me Gabby. Not Gabriele or Gabriella. Just Gabby. Like John Wayne's bowlegged, bearded, crusty old Western trail hand sidekick George "Gabby" Hayes. Somehow my mother thought Gabby was the perfect name for a little girl. (This, of course, was long before the tragic shooting of Arizona Congresswoman Gabrielle "Gabby" Giffords popularized the name, making it synonymous with courage and heroism.)

I don't think she really gave it much thought, but I'm certain that it was her idea. My father, if he had his way, would have named me Jamie, or more sensibly, after his mother, Molly, his sister, Dollie, or perhaps even his diminutive aunts, Clara or Essie.

I sometimes wonder what the hell my mother was thinking, setting me up for a lifetime of "quit your gabbing" or being called "The Gabster" or simply "Gabs." Just another reason why I'm glad I was a boy. I could live with being teasingly called "Skippy" in kindergarten, after the mid-'60s Australian TV show about a boy and his bush kangaroo. Or even the popular peanut butter sandwich spread. The occasional "kippered herring" reference barely registered as much as a peep of protest from me. All because I could have been named Gabby.

So how did I end up with the name Kipp, which sounds vaguely British? Like Gabby, it's also not exactly the most traditional sounding of Jewish names. Some think that because I was born on October 7 there must be a connection to the fall observance of Yom Kippur. Not so.

A few have speculated that it has something to do with the yarmulke (skullcap) worn by observant Jews, also known as a kippah (which, incidentally, is what my Uncle Irving in Fairlawn, New Jersey, has called me all my life — his pronunciation for "Kipper"). Not even close.

A fundamentalist Christian Korean girl in college once offered a possible explanation in the form of a pun after first hearing my name: "Keep ... You keep the truth." But that was probably her subtle attempt at proselytizing (or flirting?).

The truth is there is no deep religious, spiritual, or familial significance to my name. My mother was simply watching a movie on TV late one night, noticed during the credits that one of the bit players was named Kipp, and fell in love with the name.

This was apparently a child- and pet-naming technique used by my mother, who grew up weaned on Hollywood movies. My middle brother Drew was named after the Richard Long character in the 1946 Claudette Colbert drama *Tomorrow is Forever*. Unfortunately, my mother cannot remember the name of my eponymous movie. I have yet to discover what movie my brother Josh was named after.

How my mother came up with the name Gabby, though, is anyone's guess and remains a mystery, for there are no Gabbys in our family tree. One possibility is that my parents were friends in the mid-'60s with the renowned lyricist Jerry Leiber (of Leiber and Stoller fame) and his first wife, Gaby, a German-American actress who spoke with a heavy German accent. Gaby had famously portrayed a sexy, blonde, waif seductress in the 1955 Mickey Spillane film noir classic *Kiss Me Deadly*, my mother most likely had seen. Or perhaps it was a Gabby Hayes Western, after all.

I do know that my mother went to see Alfred Hitchcock's *Psycho* following its opening in August 1960 — two months prior to my birth — which probably explains a few things. I've always had mother issues. Thankfully, she didn't name me Norman.

According to the Oxford English Dictionary, Kipp has an old English origin and literally means "toward the pointed hill or knoll," conjuring up Brontean images of rugged Scottish Highlands or misty Moorish promontories — not exactly the birthplace of many a Jew other than, I suppose, George Eliot's Daniel Deronda.

My parents grew up far from the bucolic British countryside, amid the teeming melting pots of Depression-era Brooklyn and the Bronx. My brothers and I were raised in rustic Glen Cove, a picturesque hamlet along the North Shore of Long Island, about an hour outside of Manhattan.

I suspect that my mother subconsciously sought to Anglicize my name, along with our surroundings, for we were just about the only Jews living in Glen Cove in the early '60s. ("Hmmm? Kipp Friedman? What is your family's crest? The gefilte fish?") If that's the case, I think it would have been more effective if she had named me Heathcliff, after the Sir Laurence Olivier role in *Wuthering Heights* (another of my mother's favorite films), which would have made me the world's first (and only) Heathcliff Friedman. In some circles, Kipp is short for Cliff or Clifford, thus validating the Heathcliff connection.

I'd like to think my parents chose Adam as my middle name in a moment of guilt, just in case anyone doubted my Jewish heritage. They also held a *bris* (ritual circumcision) in our house several days after my birth, perhaps relenting to pressure from my grandparents and aunts and uncles since my older brothers had had a more subdued nonsectarian procedure in the hospital.

My *bris*, however, was upstaged by several occurrences: first, our grey Maltese cat Piper (named after Piper Laurie, another of my mother's favorite Hollywood actors; years later, she would name our black Labrador retriever Miranda after Carmen Miranda) was found gorging on the chopped liver and smoked fish that had been set out on the buffet table, and then my oldest brother Josh and cousin Robert disrupted the service, coming downstairs with their faces covered in black boot polish like Al Jolson in *The Jazz Singer*, adding a comic twist to the otherwise somber ritual.

For most of my childhood I was neutral about my name, but there was a time — especially in my impressionable early teens — when I contemplated changing it to a more common name, like Andrew, after my second cousin who was also a school friend.

Kipp just sounded too WASP-y and literary. People named Kipp hung out with people named Biff, Chad, and Chip. It made me think of the character "Pip" in *Great Expectations* and was somewhat reminiscent of the celebrated English poet and writer Rudyard Kipling. Sports stars named Kipp were in short supply, save for the Kenyan Olympic gold medalist and long-distance running star Kipchoge "Kip" Keino. I found, however, that there was a preponderance of male hair salons in the New York area with my name (usually spelled with one "p").

In the early '70s, my parents took us to see a double billing of newly restored versions of *Frankenstein* and *Dracula* at the Kip's Bay Theatre in Manhattan, and I felt a renewed sense of pride in my name, which, apparently, represented an entire East Side neighborhood.

For a time, Drew and Josh used to also call me "Flip Kipson" or "Mr. Flip" after the '70s comedian and TV star Flip Wilson, whose cross-dressing alter ego, Geraldine, famously quipped: "The devil made me do it!"

In the mid-'70s, my family started eating at the new Gaylord's Indian restaurant, which had arrived from London and singlehandedly triggered the explosion of Indian restaurants in Manhattan. Whenever we visited the restaurant, the turbaned Hindu maître d' would address me with great fanfare as "Mr. Kips." Drew found this fawning attention amusing and would repeat in an Indian accent: "Good evening, Mr. Kips" or "How are you today, Mr. Kips?" and would continue to occasionally refer to me as "Mr. Kips" — even without the Indian accent — into adulthood.

My name took a surprising new turn in high school when my friend Ron "Dustin" Hoffman gave me the nickname "Kippstein," and the name stuck. In one stroke, Ron, also known as "Dodo" — after the goofy, flightless, long-extinct bird — had managed to make my name sound more Jewish. Ron, who was about as secular a Jew as they came, would later become a *Baal Teshuva* (born-again Jew) in the mid-'80s, winding up at an Orthodox enclave in Monsey, New York, before moving to a yeshiva in Israel. Last I heard, Ron was somewhere in Austria selling commercial real estate.

Over the years I've been called many things: Kipp, Kippah, Kipper, Kippela, Kippy, Keep, Kipling, Mr. Kips, Mr. Flip, Flip Kipson, The Kippster, and even Kippstein. No matter how I'm addressed, I have grown accustomed to my name and have learned to enjoy its uniqueness.

Just don't call me Skippy. Or Gabby.

12. Paging Bela Lugosi Jr.

What do you say when Groucho Marx greets you at his front door? "Hello, Groucho!" or "What's the secret woid, Mr. Marx?"?

That was my dilemma while standing next to my father and two older brothers when we arrived at Groucho's home deep in the Hollywood Hills. It was the summer of 1975, I was fourteen, and I had grown up watching Marx Brothers movies and *You Bet Your Life* reruns on TV. We had been invited by Groucho's companion and, some say, Svengali-like business manager Erin Fleming, who had assembled a small gathering of friends for an informal dinner party.

We were living in a rented Malibu beachfront home for the summer while my father was working on two TV sitcom projects when we received the invitation to Groucho's. Apparently, Fleming had been holding regular dinner parties at Groucho's house for many admiring entertainment industry fans and longtime friends of the aging comic genius. Fleming said Groucho especially enjoyed the company of writers. When my father told her that we were staying with him, she invited us as well, noting that "Groucho loves kids." My brothers and I weren't so sure, but were thrilled to go along anyway.

Looking frail and elderly following several strokes, Groucho, at eighty-five, shuffled through the massive front door of his home to greet us. He was dressed in a pair of shorts (which revealed his bandy legs), a tropical shirt, beret, and silver orthopedic Apollo-astronaut-like slippers that were given to him as a present by officials at NASA.

Tall and slender, Fleming, a minor actress about fifty years his junior, looked elegant in an evening gown and high heels. Many credit her with revitalizing Groucho's career late in life, but detractors (including Groucho's son, Arthur) accused her of exploiting him, forcing him to work exhausting gigs despite his advanced age and declining health, to further her own ambitions.

Perhaps sensing our nervousness, Groucho helped break the tension. "It's a pleasure to meet you, Mr. Friedman," he said in a weak voice and with a deadpan expression. "You have three lovely daughters."

All that was missing was a tweak from his cigar. My brothers and I had fairly long hair at the time. Grinning from ear to ear, we each shook Groucho's hand gently (I forgot what I was going to say, and instead mumbled something) and walked in for one of the most memorable, and surreal, evenings of my life.

******

After *Steambath* was broadcast on PBS in the greater New York area in 1973, surpassing viewership on all three major TV networks, executives from CBS invited my father out to Hollywood to discuss turning his Off-Broadway hit play into a sitcom. Fresh on the heels of the success of *All in the Family* (featuring an angry, bigoted white male) and its spinoff, *Maude* (showcasing an outspoken, politically liberated woman), CBS seemed confident enough to take on God, literally — or, at least, my father's satirical take on theology.

The play depicted a steambath as a sort of purgatory and God as a Puerto Rican attendant who capriciously controls the world from his mop and bucket. CBS executives envisioned a wacky new comedy series, led by an edgy, wisecracking Hispanic star, with a different cast of characters (albeit dead) passing through the steambath each week.

(Within a few years *Chico and the Man,* starring the American comedian of Puerto Rican and German descent, Freddie Prinze — minus the dead people and thorny theological issues, and substituting a service station for the steambath/afterlife — would basically fulfill the show's promise on the rival NBC network, although *Steambath* would eventually become a minor hit series in the early '80s on the fledgling Showtime network.)

My father quickly accepted CBS's invitation to come to Hollywood. He even magnanimously agreed to waive his fee for the exploratory trip. He'd been taking trips to the West Coast to work on one project or another since the mid-'60s, always returning to New York looking as if he'd been on a spa vacation — tan and robust and brimming with health, typically bragging about the freshness of the California orange juice, which he could never seem to find in New York. He had one simple request of the CBS executives: that they agree to cover the cost of housing our family as a sort of working vacation. My brothers and I had joined him on memorable individual brief working trips to Hollywood and Las Vegas in the past, so why not take the entire family on a more extended working vacation?

My parent's marriage was in tatters at the time and he may have seen this as a last-ditch opportunity for another attempt at reconciliation;

family vacations to exotic locales were always a bright spot in their otherwise rocky marriage. Delighted, CBS readily accepted this arrangement, thinking that they had struck a bargain.

So, in early 1973, off we went on an all-expenses-paid junket, courtesy of CBS, ensconced in an opulent Hollywood bungalow on the grounds of the Beverly Hills Hotel & Bungalows, soaking in the warmth and glow of Southern California while my father toiled daily at nearby CBS studios in Burbank. What executives at CBS failed to take into consideration were the rapacious appetites of three healthy, growing teenage boys on an unlimited food expense account, not to mention my mother's insatiable shopping habits (she quickly discovered the nearby Rodeo Drive shopping district, where she returned each day loaded with oversized shopping bags under her arms like a triumphant great game hunter — only her trophies came from Chanel, Tiffany & Co., Cartier, and Hermes).

We called on room service at all hours of the day and night. Being the youngest, I was more of a burger, fries, and chocolate shake man. However, I quickly developed a fondness for Belgian waffles and French toast. I also discovered the joys of ice cream parfaits which, to me, were just overpriced ice cream sundaes, only served in a fancy tall glass. My older brothers had more refined tastes, exploring different cuts of steak on the menu, as well as bagels and lox, bacon and eggs, a variety of omelettes, fresh squeezed orange juice (of course), plus an assortment of side dishes.

I remember being so stuffed one evening that I fell sound asleep around 7:00 p.m., leaving my brothers locked out of the bungalow. They pounded on the door for a while, then gave up in frustration and decided on a different course of action. Needless to say, hotel security was not pleased when they discovered my brothers climbing in through the side window.

It took my brothers over an hour to rouse me from a catatonic slumber. First they tried shouting at me, then they shook my shoulders. When that didn't work, they resorted to pouring cold water on my face. I finally came to, refreshed and wondering why my face and pillow were wet. Our parents were out for the evening, and my brothers thought I'd died in my sleep while on their watch.

By the end of our one-week stay, when CBS executives caught wind of the mounting bill, they regretted their agreement not to pay my father a set fee, even calling into question our excessive use of room service. The final staggering tally, according to my father (who tends to exaggerate), was around $10,000, which, in today's dollars, is equivalent to $50,000. My father didn't seem to mind, though, even quipping that some poor studio executive's head would probably roll because of the exorbitant expenditure. He jokingly said that my brothers and I were probably placed on a permanent CBS blacklist from any future all-expenses-paid junkets.

******

Midway through our meal, my father leaned over to Groucho, who sat at the head of a great table absently picking at his chicken, and asked him if he could sum up what was so special about Marilyn Monroe. Groucho had been mostly silent throughout the meal, with Erin doting on him like a proud parent, cutting his food and occasionally planting a kiss on his forehead. Still, Groucho would perk up from time to time, offering an amusing rejoinder when the opportunity presented itself.

We all leaned in closely to hear the comic legend's answer, as though hanging on the words of a beloved Hasidic rebbe. My father wanted to know whether he could sense Monroe's greatness while working with her on the 1949 film *Love Happy,* which helped launch her career to stardom in Hollywood. Groucho had once described his perfect woman as someone who looks like Marilyn Monroe and talks like George S. Kaufman.

Groucho listened thoughtfully and, without missing a beat, responded: "She had great tits," and went back to eating his chicken.

******

Hollywood presented a fantasy-like world for me and my family on our half-dozen trips out West during the late '60s through the mid-'70s. The visits usually coincided with my father's work on screenplays and TV show pilots that never seemed to go anywhere. (Although the work would set the stage for his future success as a screenwriter with *Stir Crazy* in 1980, followed by *Splash* in 1984. The latter garnered him an Academy Award nomination that year for Best Original Screenplay.)

After my father had ended his affiliation with Magazine Management Co. in New York in the mid-'60s to pursue his full-time writing career, Hollywood studio executives started calling with offers of screenplays and TV pilots, at fees unheard of as an editor. No longer gainfully employed, but with a wife and three sons and a mortgage, he was eager to snap up the work as if it were found money. Living a Technicolor fantasy existence in the lap of luxury all seemed to be part of the package during those years.

An extended family vacation in a Beverly Hills Hotel bungalow was just one of those welcome perks. Howard Hughes himself was known to be a frequent guest of the iconic hotel for over thirty years, once even taking residence, simultaneously, in no less than four of the exclusive bungalows. For all we knew we may have been staying in one of Hughes's former bungalows. We spent most days lounging poolside, marveling at the mansions that dotted Sunset Boulevard in Beverly Hills, swimming in the ocean at nearby Venice Beach, and exploring downtown Hollywood.

Everything about Los Angeles seemed exotic, fresh, and unfamiliar, from the palm tress that dotted the boulevards to the West Coast TV shows and commercials. Each morning, my brothers and I sat glued to the TV, watching endless hours of Tex Avery cartoons from the 1940s and '50s, as well as episodes of Hopalong Cassidy Westerns from the '50s and the colorful Lucha Libre Spanish-language wrestling shows broadcast from Mexican stations just across the border.

We even enjoyed the ubiquitous, hokey "Go See Cal" auto dealership commercials. Cowboy auto dealer Cal Worthington became a familiar figure in his ten-gallon hat, performing outrageous stunts on his lot like riding elephants and walking pigs on a leash. The cheesy commercials ran continually and featured the mantra-like theme song set to the tune of "If You're Happy and You Know It!" The commercials burrowed their way into our heads like an earworm and soon had us singing: "If you need a better car, go see Cal …"

During our stay in the Beverly Hills Hotel bungalow, we paid a visit to our Uncle Don in his new condo development in nearby Culver City. This was the first time we had seen our uncle and cousins since they had left Franklin Square in Queens, New York, in the late '60s. A CPA and tax attorney, Uncle Don was a lifelong Brooklyn

Dodgers fan, and once the Dodgers left for Los Angeles it was only a matter of time before he would follow his beloved team out West.

Uncle Don had always been a button-downed, straight-laced kind of guy, but the glitz of Los Angeles had had an obvious impact even on him. He gave us a tour of their still-undeveloped property, including the communal pool, which had not yet been filled.

After the tour, my uncle was eager to show off the crowning jewel of his home: the brand new synchronized track lighting system. While eating my cousin Bennett's de-thawed bar mitzvah ice cream cake, my uncle entertained us with a light show of swirling yellows, oranges, blues, and reds across the living room walls. One corner of his living room was magically transformed into a miniature discotheque. The crisscrossing colors reminded me of the amorphous psychedelic shapes on movie theater screens before the curtain goes up.

My brothers and I were more impressed by the fact that Culver City was the location for much of the outdoor footage used in the Depression-era *Our Gang* and *Little Rascals* short movies, which we had watched on TV. We kept asking if they could show us any spots where *Little Rascals* episodes were shot. Our uncle, however, didn't share in our enthusiasm for this little-known bit of Hollywood trivia and seemed disappointed by our lukewarm reaction to the groovy track lighting system.

I never quite got over the grandeur of the mission-revival style Beverly Hills Hotel, with its distinctive, instantly recognizable pink-and-green motifs. Known as "the Pink Palace," the hotel reminded me of pictures I'd seen of Hearst Castle. Sky-high palm trees and immaculately manicured verdant gardens featuring bougainvillea, banana plants, and other tropical flora surrounded the twelve-acre compound. The air was heavy with the scent from nearby lemon trees and the sounds of chirping birds.

Unlike other more modern and contemporary hotels in the area such as the Beverly Wilshire, the Bel Air, and the Century Plaza, the Beverly Hills Hotel had its own understated, Old Hollywood charm. When not calling on room service, we ate meals in the storied Polo Lounge and wandered the extensive hotel gardens and palm-tree-lined streets along Sunset Boulevard. One morning, Drew and I even spotted Milton Berle, who had pulled up to the curb in a vintage Rolls-Royce, looking ever the movie star in a fedora, a silk ascot tie, and with a trademark cigar in his mouth.

The hotel even looked like a Hollywood set, as though it were locked in a time capsule from the 1930s — one could easily imagine Clark Gable and Carole Lombard pulling into the sweeping driveway in a Rolls-Royce. The professional staff, no strangers to the constant flow of celebrities and dignitaries who regularly passed through its doors, might be extras in a movie. I remember watching Svend Peterson, the lion-maned, tan Danish-American pool manager work his charm, dispensing fresh towels while captaining a team of ever-vigilant young pool attendants. Barrel-chested and muscular, he resembled a modern-day Johnny Weissmuller as he attended to the needs of star-powered hotel patrons and guests. It's no wonder that he would make several cameo appearances in movies and on TV, although the pool area was where he truly reigned supreme.

******

Dennis Wilson, the drummer for the Beach Boys, arrived late for dinner with a girlfriend in tow. He introduced himself to Groucho at the table. Groucho probably had no idea who the famous rock star was who had appeared so suddenly out of the blue. Others at the dinner table, besides my father and two older brothers, included Elliott Gould, Groucho's nephew Bill Marx (Harpo's adopted son), Erin Fleming, and a minor female pop star whose name escapes me, who had been playing the piano alongside Bill Marx earlier in the evening. Wilson had long, stringy blond hair and a scruffy beard, and most likely appeared to be a hippie to Groucho.

"It's a great honor to meet you, sir," Wilson said politely, crouching down at the table to shake Groucho's frail hand.

"Well, it oughta be," said Groucho with feigned chagrin, and went on picking at his chicken.

Wilson's face lit up in a huge smile.

******

I must have stayed at the Beverly Hills Hotel at least three or four times in the early '70s. Each time, my father had a habit of pointing out actors, producers, directors, agents, and others associated with the entertainment industry that happened to be staying at the landmark hotel, as if he were an ornithologist identifying rare species of birds. That was best-selling author Sidney Sheldon sitting next to me getting a haircut in the hotel barbershop, he casually noted one day.

My father would read the *Daily Variety* trade magazine poolside to keep tabs on the movie industry, which is where I first became familiar with such terms as whether a film was "boffo" at the box office. He followed opening weekend film box office grosses the way most people read baseball standings, speculating on the

Byzantine-like rising and sagging fortunes of film studios and studio heads. He would often have in his possession a stack of film and TV manuscripts, which most likely identified him as a "player" in Hollywood.

The Beverly Hills Hotel was my father's favorite place to stay in Los Angeles, and, with his writer's eye for detail, he was acutely aware of the hotel's daily nuances. For instance, he told us that struggling, opportunistic actors would sometimes arrange to have their names paged — sandwiched between legitimate announcements for such luminaries as Warren Beatty or Elizabeth Taylor — hoping to be discovered by Hollywood moguls known to populate the hotel pool's cabanas, chaise lounges, and the famous Polo Lounge. These were the days before cell phones, so having your name announced over the intercom was a viable public relations tactic.

One sunny day — they were all sunny days — I heard a bizarre announcement over the pool's loudspeaker: "Paging Bela Lugosi Jr. Paging Bela Lugosi Jr." A few heads turned, and even the befuddled operator did a verbal double take: "Hey, wait a min —" but otherwise the announcement went unanswered. Bela Lugosi had been dead for over twenty years, and not many knew he had a namesake.

About a minute later came another announcement: "Paging Lon Chaney Jr. Paging Lon Chaney Jr." Lon Chaney Jr. was then in his late sixties and living in relative obscurity in California, following years of debilitating alcoholism (he would die later that year of a massive heart attack).

Another message soon followed: "Paging Tor Johnson. Paging Tor Johnson." Tor Johnson was a hulking, bald former Swedish wrestler who played bit parts in B-grade horror movies, most famously as

"Lobo," the police-inspector-turned-zombie in *Plan 9 from Outer Space,* which many critics consider the worst film ever made. Johnson, too, had been dead for several years, but his memory had been kept alive in the pages of *Famous Monsters of Filmland* magazine.

By this time, I knew it was my older brothers, Josh and Drew, having some fun at poolside. They kept dialing the operator and disguising their voice so they could page their favorite celebrities, both dead and alive.

Next came: "Paging Tom Carvel," the octogenarian founder of the Carvel ice cream empire, known for cheesy TV commercials promoting "rum baba nut cake" and other ice cream specials back home in the New York area.

Of course, they couldn't leave out their heroes, The Three Stooges: "Paging Dr. Howard. Dr. Howard. Dr. Fine." Then came "Paging Bud Abbott," the ultimate straight man in the Abbott and Costello classic comedy duo. Abbott had died within the past week, and my brothers saw this as a fitting tribute to their fallen hero. They had hoped that there was some clueless person at poolside who hadn't heard about his death. Eventually my brothers grew bored, or the hotel switchboard caught on, and their gag announcements stopped.

During one visit to Los Angeles, our family had dinner with Bea Arthur, who was at the height of her TV *Maude* fame. Arthur and her then-husband Gene Saks, a film and stage director of many Neil Simon plays, including *The Odd Couple,* lived in a charming modern home in nearby Brentwood Estates. I had last seen Arthur back in 1968 when I was seven and we had traveled to Baltimore for the weekend to see a musical adaptation of my father's best-selling novel, *A Mother's Kisses.* Saks was the director of that production and they hoped to take the musical all the way to Broadway. (Sadly, it closed in Baltimore.)

In the musical, Arthur played an overbearing New York Jewish mother who follows her son to college in the Midwest. I don't remember specifics of what was discussed over dinner, but her own overbearing nature, which made her perfect for the role, was certainly in full flourish that night. I can still hear her raspy, mannish voice and picture her large hands and wide-set shoulders. She was tough, intimidating — and I got the impression that she didn't care much for the presence of three teens, either. She reminded me of my late paternal grandmother, Nanny, in the Bronx, who was also blessed with an acid wit and a gravelly voice but who was not particularly warm toward children. Nevertheless, at twelve, I was more interested in the roast beef and Yorkshire pudding than all their talk of movies, TV, and the theater — and soon after dessert, I passed out on the couch.

******

During dessert, my brother Josh asked Groucho if he remembered the Playhouse Theater in Great Neck, Long Island. Groucho had once lived in Great Neck in the '20s, where he lost his fortune overnight during the Great Depression, before moving out to Hollywood to revitalize his career. Josh pointed out that our family had also lived in Great Neck, in the late '60s, and he asked Groucho if he remembered whether the Playhouse was used for vaudevillian acts. To help jog Groucho's memory, he said that the theater still had an original old organ below the front stage.

Without missing a beat, Groucho chimed in: "I have an old organ myself."

******

My first brush with Hollywood actually occurred years earlier in the south of France in the summer of 1965. My family had rented a villa in Juan-les-Pins along the French Riviera, following the success of my father's bestselling novel, *A Mother's Kisses*. We spent our days at the Hotel Du Cap-Eden-Roc Antibes resort along the seashore. Josh, at nine, took a stab at cliff diving, while Drew learned to swim with his French instructor, substituting the words "New York, France" for "left, right."

One day, while I was playing in the children's wading pool, a bald, tanned man with a pot belly and sunglasses approached, holding the hand of a little boy about my age. He asked if I would like to play with his son. I looked up and said "no" and resumed playing by myself.

My middle-aged babysitter, Mrs. Sullivan, who sat nearby in a large sundress, wide-brimmed hat, and dark cat-eyed sunglasses to protect her fair, freckled skin from the Mediterranean sun, gave me a reproachful "Kippy!"

Undeterred, the man said in a commanding voice, with an accent that reminded me of Bela Lugosi's Dracula: "Look at me with those big brown eyes."

I looked up and grudgingly agreed to play with his son. A few years later, I would recognize the man as "Mr. Freeze" in the *Batman* TV series, as well as the Nazi prisoner-of-war-camp warden in the Academy Award-winning movie *Stalag 17*. Otto Preminger, the famed actor/director, had been vacationing with his family at the Hotel Du Cap-Eden-Roc that summer between movie shoots.

Later that summer, Mrs. Sullivan would have her own brush with fame while on a weekend trip by herself to Italy. She ran into John

Wayne, of all people, outside her hotel in Rome. Ever the gentleman, the Duke would literally sweep her off her feet, giving her a warm embrace and a peck on the cheek, even calling her a "little lady," thus providing her with the thrill of a lifetime. Mrs. Sullivan was like a blushing schoolgirl whenever she related that story to us. It was hard to imagine my heavy-set, middle-aged babysitter in the arms of the film legend, but such is the magic and allure of Hollywood.

I first visited Hollywood in 1969 when I was nine. I can't recall what project my father was working on — he always seemed to be juggling a number of them at once — but I know that he was asked around that time to write a pilot for a spin-off of the TV show *That Girl,* featuring Marlo Thomas's befuddled boyfriend Donald Hollinger, played by Ted Bessell. The pilot would be called *The Ted Bessell Show* (a few pilot episodes were actually shot and aired, but the show didn't take off).

The previous year, my father had taken Drew to Hollywood while working briefly on a screenplay for an adaptation of the Broadway hit play "The Owl and the Pussycat," which would eventually be made into a hit romantic comedy starring Barbra Streisand and George Segal in 1970, with Buck Henry given the screenwriting credit. Drew and my father stayed in a bungalow at the Beverly Hills Hotel while my father worked on the screenplay at nearby Columbia Pictures Studios.

One day he brought Drew along with him to the home of the film's producer, Ray Stark, who lived in a mansion in Beverly Hills that was previously owned by Humphrey Bogart — a fact that didn't really impress my brother, who mostly brooded during his trip. He sorely missed his guinea pig, his television set, and his bedroom back home. He was equally unimpressed when told that Stark's mother-in-law was the legendary actress and comedienne Fanny Brice. He perked up, however, when he was allowed to explore Stark's massive library and discovered a book about monster movies entitled *The Illustrated History of Horror Films,* which he also owned.

I was more interested in plying Drew for information about the wonders of Disneyland (which was also a letdown for him). My only experience with Disneyland was limited to watching *The Wonderful World of Disney* show on Sunday nights.

My trip to Hollywood with my father got off to a bumpy start. I got sick on the flight, but thankfully the in-flight movie, plus my *Mad Libs* booklets, made the five-hour journey more endurable. Around midnight, we pulled into the Century Plaza Hotel in Century City in a Hertz gold-colored Pontiac Firebird with the license plate that I had already, in my youthful exuberance, committed to memory: ZQW-107.

With its sweeping, crescent-shaped frontage and spectacular fountains, the majestic nineteen-story hotel building resembled the United Nations building back home in New York. My father made a point of telling me how the hotel was already a personal favorite of President Nixon's as well as of a host of visiting dignitaries', including Moshe Dayan, and of such celebrities as Bob Hope. I was more impressed by the doormen, who greeted us in red Beefeater costumes. I was also amazed to discover the "After Eight Thin Mints" that magically appeared on our pillowcases each night. My father noted that President Nixon also was a secret admirer of the hotel's thin, chocolate-covered mints.

During our weekend in Southern California, we visited Disneyland, and the whole experience was indeed more magical than I could imagine. We even had time to visit the Marineland of the Pacific park and aquarium along the ocean, enjoying splashing killer whale shows as well as dolphins, sea lions, and harbor seals that bounced beachballs from their snouts. My father tried to keep me busy during the day, taking me to tourist sites along Sunset Boulevard, including Grauman's Chinese Theater and a novelty shop where I purchased a starter magic kit.

He even took me to some of his favorite restaurants, including Steer's on La Cienega Boulevard, which specialized in prime rib. He noted that he liked the ease with which the races mixed at the restaurant — something that would not have been as prevalent back in New York. A cheerful young waitress with a nametag, who spoke in a folksy Midwestern twang, announced that she would be our server.

"My, you're quite a cupcake," my father greeted her, causing her to blush.

For a moment, I thought of calling her a cupcake, too.

As much as I enjoyed my trips to Los Angeles, there was always an air of unreality. This was my father's playground — a place where he could get away from the real world struggles and stress back home in New York. Not once did I ever wonder what it would be like to actually live in Los Angeles, even when I spent most of the summer of 1975 living in Malibu. It just didn't seem like a city at all.

Unlike New York, with all roads leading to the familiar Manhattan skyline, L.A. was instead pockets of communities spread out along a never-ending highway. What I did see of downtown West Hollywood reminded me of continuous strip malls.

The only time it felt somewhat familiar was at night, when the Hollywood Strip lit up like a West Coast, tropical version of New

York's Times Square. Colorful billboard signs advertised the latest movies and rock stars. Large neon signs seemed to be everywhere. The one that stood out to me was Dino's Lodge, a nightclub owned by Dean Martin. The thought of having Dean Martin as your neighbor, collecting the morning paper in a bathrobe and slippers, just didn't seem right. Like much of Hollywood, Dino was larger than life. He belonged on neon billboard signs, movie screens — or at least on your TV set.

******

Following dinner, Groucho retired to his bedroom and returned a few minutes later dressed in a bathrobe, still wearing his NASA slippers. He looked like he was ready for bed. He stood by the dining room entrance alongside Erin. They were soon flanked by two of the wait staff: a pretty blonde and a brunette, each dressed in sexy black French maid outfits, complete with feather dusters, looking like Frederick's of Hollywood catalogue models.

Groucho's nephew Bill Marx had made his way over to the piano. Groucho proceeded to perform a thirty-minute medley of Marx Brothers classic movie songs, including "Hooray for Captain Spaulding," "Hello, I Must Be Going," "Oh, How That Woman Could Cook," "Father's Day," and "Show Me a Rose." Erin filled in admirably, doing the Margaret Dumont straight parts while Groucho hammed it up.

He sang in a thin voice that grew stronger as the impromptu performance continued. I felt like I was watching *Duck Soup* and *Animal Crackers* all over again. Energized by our enthusiastic response, Groucho managed to rekindle some of that old Marx Brothers magic. He kicked his ankles backward, rolled his eyes, tilted his head in a swoon, and even shimmied his waist.

The highlight for me was when he carried out a modified version of his famous chicken-walking lope, with one hand on the small of his back, while singing "Lydia, the Tattooed Lady." We were all awestruck, and we applauded generously.

The guests started to leave soon after the medley of show tunes was over. We were preparing to go as well when Groucho and Erin invited us on a quick tour of their home. They led us past hallways covered with Marx Brothers memorabilia documenting Groucho's remarkable career. Pictures showed Groucho's humble Upper East Side beginnings, when he and his brothers were known as "Minnie's Boys." There were shots from old vaudevillian acts. Framed movie posters dotted the walls. Other pictures showed them gagging with Hollywood studio heads, U.S. Presidents, heads of state. It was a who's who of some of the greatest comedians and celebrities of the twentieth century.

Our tour eventually led us to his bedroom, where Groucho slept on a large wooden bed that had been constructed from the remains of a wagon that had belonged to his grandparents in the Old Country. My father had brought along a copy of his novel, *The Dick,* and quickly wrote an inscription made out to Groucho.

Groucho retrieved a paperback copy of his memoir, *Groucho and Me,* from a shelf and jotted down an inscription to my father. After exchanging books, they hugged and then Erin tucked Groucho in bed and led us away. When we got into our car to drive away, my father opened Groucho's memoir and read aloud the inscription: "To Bruce. Nothing in this book will harm you. Groucho."

A few days later, Erin invited us back for another dinner at Groucho's. This time, the guest of honor would be Mae West, whom Groucho hadn't seen in decades.

To our everlasting regret, for some reason, we declined this historic reunion of comedy legends.

Afterword

by Josh Alan Friedman

If, for some strange reason, someone were to read my own *Black Cracker,* my father's *Lucky Bruce,* and Kipp's *Barracuda in the Attic,* they would assume each took place in a separate universe. They did. And yet these versions of life all coexisted in our daily routine. Long Island is awfully big, and the whole idea of it has yet to be fully defined. It sure didn't feel like an island. It went on forever, and I still hear names of towns I never knew existed.

As such, I never knew (until now) what was going on in Kipp's neck of the woods. With five years' difference in age, we never shared the business of school. It was a revelation that he considered me heroic, if for one shining moment, when I whipped some guy in the snow who had bullied him. I'd do it again today, but the kid can take care of himself. He was always a tough, scrappy athlete. Whenever we sparred with souvenir boxing gloves in the den, no punch could faze him and he kept on coming.

Recently I saw my younger, Midwestern brother in action. I watched how smoothly he manned his desk, making things come to life around a local event in Milwaukee. He used the telephone like a gentleman of the press from a bygone era. Arranging lunches, photos, radio spots. Whether dealing with Milwaukee politicians, police, or newsrooms, all were eager to take his call, and results were swift and easy. Good will all around.

That is who the little boy in this book became.